Politics by principle, not interest

Politics by principle, not interest
Toward nondiscriminatory democracy

JAMES M. BUCHANAN

George Mason University

ROGER D. CONGLETON

George Mason University

CAMBRIDGE
UNIVERSITY PRESS

PUBLISHED BY THE PRESS SYNDICATE OF THE UNIVERSITY OF CAMBRIDGE
The Pitt Building, Trumpington Street, Cambridge CB2 1RP, United Kingdom

CAMBRIDGE UNIVERSITY PRESS
The Edinburgh Building, Cambridge CB2 2RU, United Kingdom
40 West 20th Street, New York, NY 10011-4211, USA
10 Stamford Road, Oakleigh, Melbourne 3166, Australia

First published 1998

Printed in the United States of America

Typeset in Times Roman

Library of Congress Cataloging-in-Publication Data

Buchanan, James M.
    Politics by principle, not interest : toward nondiscriminatory
democracy / James M. Buchanan, Roger D. Congleton.
        p.   cm.
    ISBN 0-521-62187-9 (hardcover)
    1. Equality.   2. Justice.   3. Majorities.   4. Discrimination.
    5. Social choice.   I. Congleton, Roger D.   II. Title.
    JC578.B83   1998   97-40983
    320′.01′1 – dc21   CIP

A catalog record for this book is available from
the British Library

ISBN 0 521 62187 9 hardback

[The First Amendment] ought to read, "Congress shall make no law authorizing government to take any discriminatory measures of coercion." I think that would make all the other rights unnecessary, and it creates the sort of conditions I would want to see.

– Friedrich A. Hayek in a videotaped interview with James M. Buchanan,
28 October 1978

Contents

List of figures and tables

Figures

Tables

Preface

"Politics by principle" is that which modern politics is not. What we observe is "politics by interest," whether in the form of explicitly discriminatory treatment (rewarding or punishing) of particular groupings of citizens or of some elitist–*dirigiste* classification of citizens into the deserving and nondeserving on the basis of a presumed superior wisdom about what is really "good" for us all. The proper principle for politics is that of generalization or generality. This standard is met when political actions apply to all persons independently of membership in a dominant coalition or an effective interest group. The generality principle is violated to the extent that political action is overtly discriminatory in the sense that the effects, positive or negative, depend on personalized identification. The generality norm finds its post-Enlightenment philosophical foundation in Kant's normative precept for a personalized ethics and its institutional embodiment in the idealized rule of law that does, indeed, set out widely agreed upon criteria for the evaluation of legal structures.

In one sense, it is surprising that the generalization principle has not been applied directly to politics. But except in those settings in which politically driven action impinges upon the generality precept promoted in law, there has been little recognition of the potential relevance of the generalization norm. Such failure or oversight has been due, in large part, to the residual dominance of a romanticized and idealized vision of "the state" – an entity that remains benevolent toward its citizens while providing citizens with opportunity for full self-realization. In this vision, any principle must act to constrain the collective–political enterprise and may prevent the state from "doing good," as defined in its own omniscient discovery.

Why has the generality principle been understood to be critically important in the working of the law but relatively less significant for politics? Perhaps the recognition that "the law" must be applied in a decentralized institutional setting has partially forestalled a romanticism comparable to that which has motivated politics. Many separate judges could scarcely be deemed omnisciently benevolent to an extent necessary to generate a coherent structure of law, without which social order cannot emerge. As it develops, and as it is widely observed, law must incorporate some variant of a generalization norm; unequal treatment of like cases violates law in its basic definitional sense. By contrast, romanticized politics remains monolithic; the "good" is defined uniquely by the collective agency of the state. There need be no ultimate dispute among competing authorities.

The idealistic vision of politics has been challenged seriously, both in theory and in practice over the course of the decades after World War II. And the challenges have succeeded in bringing politics and politicians out of the obscurantist haze that characterized post-Hegelian mentality. Both in the academy and on the street, politics and politicians are now exposed to a skepticism that is reminiscent of the late eighteenth century – the period during which the constitutional principles for the politics of classical liberal order were laid down. The modern shift in public attitudes toward politics and politicians has not, however, been accompanied by a reinvigoration of constitutional discourse, aimed at imposing limits on the extended range of state activity that the two-century dominance of the romantic vision allowed to occur. There has as yet come to be no widespread understanding that a nonmonolithic, nonbenevolent, and nonomniscient politics requires an anchor in principle, lest it remain subject to the capricious forces of rotating coalitional interests.

This book is an enterprise of constitutional argument – one that is normative only to the extent that it remains informed throughout by the single principle of generality. There is no effort to lay down precise guidelines for what should and should not be done by politics. The critical distinction is procedural rather that substantive. Politics by principle constrains agents and agencies of governance to act nondiscriminatorily, to treat all persons and groups of persons alike, and to refrain from behavior that is, in its nature, selective. Within the limits of such constraints, politics may do much or little, and it may do what is done in varying ways.

We argue that our politics may be made "better" in the evaluation of all participants, if political action can be constrained constitutionally so as to meet more closely the generality norm. We acknowledge that this normative stance is based on our own positive analysis of how the politics that we observe actually works. The basic public choice model of politics that informs our whole discussion need not be accepted by all observers–analysts, and, further, differing normative inferences may be drawn, even from a commonly shared analysis.

We advance no claim of synthesis. Our scholarship is limited to what we claim to be consistent application of an internally coherent perspective to complex phenomena of social interaction. We make no effort to extend the discussion to include either detailed consideration or criticism of alternative perspectives that are acknowledged to exist. This disclaimer seems especially important for the inquiry that we undertake in this book.

In particular, we defend our willingness to publish this book against possible charges that we neglect major lines of inquiry, both precursory and parallel to our own, and notably in legal philosophy, both old and modern. The generality norm – its history, its development in application, its current standing – has long been central in the discourse of legal scholars and jurists. We acknowledge our illiteracy in front of this whole body of scholarship, but we accompany this acknowledgement by a reminder that there are advantages of specialization in intellectual–philosophical inquiry as well as in more mundane activity. As political economists, we could, at best, remain dilettantes in legal philosophy. Is it not best to reduce somewhat the sweep of our persuasive potential and to enter our admittedly restricted set of insights into the lists alongside others that may be advanced by those whose perspectives and scientific credentials differ?

When all is said and done, how is synthesis achieved? Is it not possible that synthesis emerges more or less spontaneously as the insights offered by several perspectives are advanced? Perhaps each of the blind men, having himself first described his personal experiential encounter with the reality of the elephant, arrives at some accurate comprehension of the whole beast as he integrates the accounts of others with his own. Perhaps no overarching synthesizer need arise at all.

This book has gone through a relatively long gestation period. Elements of the analytical argument were developed by Professor Buchanan in both lecture presentations and published materials as early as 1993 (Buchanan, 1993a). Extended and more technical versions of central portions of the argument were presented at the meeting of the European Public Choice Society in Valencia, Spain, in early 1994 and published in 1995 (Buchanan, 1995a). This paper closely parallels the analysis of Chapter 3, but it is more specifically organized as a basic criticism of public choice theory.

The book is jointly authored, and it is always appropriate to attempt some attribution of responsibility to the separate contributors. Professor Buchanan initially developed the central argument, as referenced earlier, and he is primarily responsible both for the introductory Chapter 1 and for the analytical chapters in Part Two. Professor Congleton joined the enterprise when prospects for a book-length presentation were initially discussed, and his primary responsibility may be identified in several of the application chapters in Part Three. More specifically, Professor Congleton prepared initial versions of Chapters 6, 10, 12, and 13 and is also a major contributor to Chapter 11. Professor Buchanan wrote the early drafts for Chapters 7, 8, and 9 as well as Chapter 11. He is also primarily responsible for the concluding Chapter 14.

Acknowledgements

The Liberty Fund conference series on Constitutional Economics, organized under the supervision of our then-colleague, Viktor Vanberg, provided the occasion for early presentations of the generality principle in a constitutional setting. Participants in these conferences, especially in 1992, were helpful in offering early support, or, at the least, in their failure to discourage the whole enterprise in its early infancy. One of the active participants in those conferences was Hartmut Kliemt, Duisburg, Germany, whom we invited in 1995–96 to review carefully the analytical corpus of the book. His careful, detailed, and fundamental criticisms prompted major revisions of the material, especially those in Chapters 4 and 5, and we should acknowledge Kliemt's assistance in preventing an embarrassing analytical "chasing of tails" that described earlier versions.

We have also found many discussions with Yong J. Yoon to be helpful, especially with reference to the logical underpinnings of the stylized models examined in Part One. We are grateful to Todd Sandler and to an anonymous reader for many detailed comments that helped us to clarify the final argument developed in this book.

Jo Ann Burgess, Archivist-Librarian at the Buchanan House, Center for Study of Public Choice, has been involved directly in every stage of the production process of this book. Her contribution is not sufficiently weighted in passing reference in the Acknowledgements.

Finally, both authors have benefited from the research environment provided by the Center for Study of Public Choice, George Mason University, under the direction of Robert Tollison and, in particular, the encouragement and support of Betty Tillman, Administrative Director of the Center, who have both remained a vital component of this as well as earlier research products of Buchanan and coauthors.

James M. Buchanan
Roger D. Congleton
Fairfax, Virginia
June 1997

PART ONE
Introduction

1   Generality, law, and politics

Social sciences analyze the relationships between and among persons, groups, and organizations. This inclusive definition incorporates economic, legal, political, and social interactions. In ordinary market exchange, the individual is simultaneously a demander and supplier, a buyer and seller. In social arrangements, the person may be both a care giver and a care receiver, a lover and a beloved, a gift taker and gift giver, a friend and a befriended. By comparison, in law and in politics such reciprocity need not be present. The individual is subject to the law, but he may or may not be a member–participant of the organized entity that makes–changes or enforces the law. In fiscal politics, the individual is subject to the coerced exaction of taxation and to the possible nonexclusive benefits of governmental programs, but he may or may not be a member–voter–participant in the collectivity that makes basic political choices. In either of these cases, in which the individual is subject to but not a participant in the process, reaction rather than explicit reciprocation describes behavior.

Our concern in this book is exclusively with those structures of social order that qualify as "democratic" in some ultimate participatory sense. We shall not analyze the relationships between individuals and an externally existing maker–enforcer of law and political authority. Critics may suggest that the authority of convention and tradition, especially in law, places any subject–person in a position that is not different, in kind, from that which is present under externally imposed rules. But the individual, as a participant in a continuing process, also plays some part in constructing the order itself. There is no basis for a classification of persons into the two permanently defined sets of subjects and rulers. In another sense, of course, the individual remains always subject to the law and to political dictates, no matter what the degree of participation. Nonetheless, "democracy," defined in terms of potential access to participation in decision structures, remains categorically different from "nondemocracy." The democratic proviso implies that each person has a voice, actual or potential, in making, changing, and enforcing the law and in generating political action under which persons, groups, and organizations behave. But membership and potential participation, as such, do not imply equality either in influence on collective choices that are made or on the separate impact of these choices on persons. The normative argument for equality along these dimensions must be based on the rational choices of members–participants themselves.

A. Are rules discovered or made?

At this point, it is necessary to make a critical distinction between two competing presuppositions as to what law and politics are – a distinction that is related to, but somewhat different from, the conflict of visions noted in the Preface. The first, which has been called a *truth judgment* conception, basically understands and describes the

3

activity of constitutional law and politics in a metaphor of discovery. That which is to be found exists independently of the process through which it comes into cognition. Persons, as members of an organized community, live together under a set of rules, under laws, and also under political–collective structures. But what brings these laws, these structures, into being? In this conception, political discourse involves a search for the "good" and the "true" for the community. And the putative claim that some members of the group are more qualified to discern the good, the true, and the beautiful is almost impossible to refute in that metaphorical setting. Surely, if that which is good exists only to be found, we must acknowledge that there may be experts whose discovery talents are relatively superior.

Note that, in this truth judgment conception, there is little or no basis for democratic equality in either of the senses mentioned. If there are members of the community who do, in fact, possess relatively superior skills in discovering that which is good, legitimately these members can be allowed relatively greater influence over any final determination. And, if that which is good for the community does, indeed, exist independently of the process of discovery itself, there seems to be no logical linkage between goodness and the distribution of effects among all of the community's members. The fundamental idea, and ideal, of measured democratic equality is self-contradictory in this setting, despite the observed juxtaposition of the discovery metaphor and the participatory ideal in the thinking of so many modern philosophers.

The opposing contractarian conception of law and politics is based squarely in the rejection of any claim that the institutions and the policies that are good for the community are "out there" waiting to be discovered by experts or anyone else. The rules for living together – the basic law and political structure – are, quite literally, made up or created in some participatory process of discussion, analysis, persuasion, and mutual agreement. In this conception of social order, the constitution, inclusively defined, emerges from agreement among those who must abide by the constraints contained within it. The constitutional stage, which involves both law and politics, is understood and described best in terms of an exchange of agreements among participating members of the community. Persons agree to constraints on their own liberties in exchange for comparable constraints being imposed on the liberties of others. The metaphor is that of a social contract. And agreement itself serves as the criterion for goodness or truth.[1] That rule or political action that is good for the community of persons is defined by that option upon which agreement is reached rather than some imagined correspondence with an independently discoverable object of community search.

Note that both the role of the expert and the place of participation become quite different from those implied in the discovery conception. There is, quite simply, little for an expert to discover in a setting where agreement itself signals success. The putative expert is forestalled from making claims to define that which is best for others. The informed observer can, at best, assist in the ongoing dialogue among participants by clarifying and articulating arguments. At this juncture, contractarian discourse finds common ground with the efforts of those philosophers, like Habermas (1983) and Ackerman (1980), who emphasize the relevance and importance of dialogue among participants.

Participation itself also occupies a categorically different place in the stylized contractarian process from that occupied in the truth judgment model. In the latter, participation as such is not important. What reason is there for every member of the community to participate in the discovery of that which exists independently of the process? Only to the extent that a many-person search offers greater assurance of ultimate success in finding the grail can universal or even extensive participation be defended. In contrast, at least as stylized, participation is the *sine qua non* of the contractarian enterprise. The exchange metaphor is convincing. How could exchange take place without participation of the traders? The expression of agreement to the terms of an exchange becomes the necessary criterion for legitimating the result.

As adherents of the contractarian conception, we acknowledge the difficulties in bridging the gap between the stylized model of the agreement process and the political–legal reality that may be observed. Persons find themselves as members of politically organized communities, and they have no sense of having participated in any explicit contract with others on the shape and form of the political–legal structure to which they are subjected. In this respect, there would seem to be relatively little difference in attitudes toward allegedly democratic structures and those that might be known to have been imposed by external authority. We suggest, nonetheless, that the justificatory enterprise becomes quite different in the two cases. Those who would mount a defense of existing constitutional structure can easily present an argument drawn from the truth judgment or discovery metaphor. "That which exists is that which is in the community's best interest, as chosen by the wisdom of the sages or the ages." To the contractarian the question posed is: Could the existing set of rules have emerged from the agreement among all parties who are currently subject to them? Or, in individualistic terms, the proper question is: Could I have agreed to the set of rules that the existing political–legal structure represents?

In approaching these questions, either as an individual or as an assessor of constitutional order, there must be a bias toward affirmation rather than rejection, if for no other reason than existence and historical development – the basis, of course, for traditional conservative evaluation. Assent is more than acquiescence, at least to the extent that an exit option exists. Perhaps it is incumbent upon the critic to treat that which exists as "relatively absolute absolutes" (Buchanan, 1989). But such bias does not equate with making current rules sacrosanct and beyond ultimate critical inquiry. And in such inquiry it is appropriate to raise the central contractarian question. Could the ordered arrangements that exist reflect agreement for all members of the body politic?

B. The uses of the veil

The contractarian enterprise is necessarily individualistic at least in a foundational sense. But who are the stylized contractors? How are the parties to the political–constitutional exchange to be described? The potential objects of agreement are constraints on the liberties of personal behavior – constraints that, presumably, will be mutually beneficial to all parties. If initially, however, persons and groups are in putative possession of endowments and goods that are differentially valued, there would seem to be differential interests in any exchange, thereby making agreement difficult if not impossible.

At the most basic constitutional level, however, the absence of agreement implies the absence of social order. No person is secure in any claim to value. It is precisely this imagined setting that led Thomas Hobbes (1943/1651) to develop his direful argument in support of the personal surrender of liberties to sovereign political authority as the only means of escape from the anarchistic war of each against all. In contraposition to Hobbes, John Locke's metaphor for the justificatory origins of political order emerged in a more stable historical epoch. Locke (1675/1689) advanced the empirical proposition to the effect that persons enter into potential political agreements already endowed with mutually acknowledged natural rights to person and property. Locke did not answer the Hobbesian question; he simply assumed that it did not arise. Political order finds its legitimacy in natural rights, the recognition of which serves also to limit the range and extension for political authority.

Elements of both the Hobbesian and the Lockean metaphors remain present in modern attitudes toward the legitimacy of existing political order in Western democratic regimes and the structure of individual claims to liberties under those regimes. But neither of these constructions, nor any combination, seems sufficient to sate the modern demand for justificatory argument. Some criterion over and beyond either the dominating motive of personal security or the presumed existence of recognized natural boundaries is needed if the ultimate legitimacy of political coercion is to be established.

Quite apart from any estimate of relative economic position, any potential participant would ideally prefer the imposition of restrictive rules on the behavior of others while remaining at liberty to follow or not to follow rules (Buchanan, 1975a). But each participant will also recognize that others will agree to impose constraints on their own behavior only as a part of a reciprocal "exchange." In this preliminary sense, reciprocation itself implies generality. Constraining rules that emerge from general agreement will tend to be *general* in application. Rules that apply to others must also be applied to one's own behavior. With relative positions clearly identified, however, different participants may place differing evaluations on alternative sets of rules, and agreement may be impossible.

The veil of ignorance and/or uncertainty offers a means of bridging the apparent gap between furtherance of separately identified interests and agreement on the rules that conceptually define the "social contract." Potential contractors must recognize that the basic rules for social order – the ultimate constitutional structure – are explicitly chosen as permanent or quasi-permanent parameters within which social interaction is to take place over a whole sequence of periods. This temporal feature, in itself, shifts discussion away from that which might take place among fully identified bargainers and toward discussion among participants who are unable to predict either their own positions or how differing rules will affect whatever positions they come to occupy. Participants may be led to examine rules from behind a "veil of ignorance" (Harsanyi, 1955; Rawls, 1971) or "uncertainty" (Buchanan and Tullock, 1962) on some presumption that identification is impossible. Criteria of fairness may replace those of advantage; agreement may emerge as the predicted working properties of alternative sets of rules are examined.

It is important to understand how and why the veil of ignorance/uncertainty places severe restrictions on the arguments in discussions among potential contracting parties – discussions that may generate some convergence toward agreement. By necessity, the person who advances an argument in support of one particular rule (or set of rules) must invoke criteria that take on elements of general or public interest. An argument may claim that this or that rule is indeed in the "general" interest (as defined by the anonymity of the veil), and that such a rule is supported, not from altruism, but from the necessary coincidence between individual and general interest.

The veil of ignorance and/or uncertainty is a construction that is helpful in some ultimate evaluation of alternative rules. The construction, as such, however, does not readily allow an objectively identifiable classification of political actions that may or may not meet the abstracted generality norm. Almost any observed political action, no matter how discriminatory in effect, may be rhetorically defended on some veil-of-ignorance argument. In order to establish the generality principle operationally, it is necessary to examine its foundations more carefully.

C. Equality under law

This book has a single theme. The argument is that the generality principle be extended to politics. But extended from what? The basis for the whole discussion involves both the recognition and normative appreciation of the operation and applicability of the generality principle in law. It may be useful to examine these legal foundations for generality briefly before plunging into the analysis of politics per se.

To this point, law and politics have not been separated in our treatment of the inclusive contractarian enterprise. The fundamental concern is with the establishment of normative legitimacy of coercion on the behavior of persons who are themselves participants in the collectivity, the organized social order. At this basic level of inquiry, law becomes a component of the comprehensive political structure. A simple law that prevents my trespass on my neighbor's property is meaningful only to the extent that violations are enforceable by the authority of the state. Further, the very existence of such a law implies some prior enactment by collective agency, or at least some collective acceptance of evolving standards of private adjudication. Nonetheless, in ordinary parlance, we do not elevate the necessary political component of law to center stage. We limit the term *politics* to the explicit current actions of state agencies in changing existing laws and, primarily, to actions involving direct operation of state enterprises, broadly defined (departments, bureaus, commissions, etc.)

In some fundamental sense, the whole of the social interaction process, including the economy, is necessarily "political," because all behavior is constrained by encompassing law that must, itself, find ultimate origin in political action or at least be backed up with fundamental coercive power. But it remains useful, nonetheless, to separate the political from the private sector of interaction, thereby relegating the embodied politics of law and legal structure to the ongoing and partially decentralized activities of jurists rather than politicians. Perhaps predictably, the dividing lines between politics and law may often be difficult to maintain, both in theory and in practice. For purposes of our discussion here, however, the significant point is that there does indeed exist a rather clear separation between politics and law when the activities are evaluated in terms of principles.

The distinction may be clarified through the introduction of a simple example. Two families occupy contiguous territories. The law of property specifies the dividing line and provides potential enforcement for violation. Each family carries on its own activity *within the law*, so long as it does not trespass. There is no politics, or political interaction, as such. Suppose now, however, that the two families share, at least potentially, in the value that might be produced by draining the adjacent meadow. There is now a necessary political relationship, whether or not it is intentionally formalized.

The very meaning of *law* implies generality in application, at least in modern democracies, and especially as legitimated by contractarian criteria. It is difficult to derive conceptual agreement on laws or rules that explicitly impact differentially on separate persons and groups. Law then becomes legitimate only if all persons could have agreed conceptually, and such agreement is most likely when all persons affected are generally and reciprocally constrained in their behavior. The law that prohibits my trespass on my neighbor's property is legitimate only because the same law prohibits her trespass on my property. Differential treatment under the operation of the law, say, on the basis of gender, age, race, religion, class, location, or political access, is to be condemned as violative of the central normative principle. To suggest that law is and must be organized on this principle of generality or equality does not, of course, carry with it any claim that the legal structure, as it operates, satisfies fully its acknowledged normative standard in this respect. It is, however, difficult to think about the practical operation of a legal structure that is not informed by the generality precept and that does not somehow embody adherence to the generality norm as an ever-present objective.[2]

The generality principle in law implies equal treatment under and by the law – equal treatment for all persons who are or may be affected by those constraints that the law defines. The principle, as such, contains no direction or implication as to the extent of behavior that is brought within the limits of the law. A social order may be described by adherence to the generality principle in legal structure even if many details of personal behavior are severely constrained. That is to say, a regime of equal liberties among all persons may or may not be a regime of extensive liberties. The intrusiveness or nonintrusiveness of law is not addressed by the generality or equality principle, as such.

D. The efficiency of generality in law

"Equal liberties under law" – we agree with John Rawls in claiming that a regime described by the presence of this condition has met the first test for contractarian justice. The contrary presence, that of "inequality under law," would not emerge from contractual agreement among affected parties, whether such agreement be actual or hypothetical. The primacy of this strictly normative argument for generality need not be challenged. But a supporting argument may be adduced – an argument that is based on efficiency in application. A legal structure that embodies equal treatment is more efficient than one that introduces inequality. Fewer resources are required to make the structure functional.

The analysis behind this proposition is straightforward. But the discussion is made difficult by the categorically different usage of the term *efficient* or *efficiency* in some variants of the modern law–economics discourse, especially those associated with the works of Richard Posner (1972). To suggest that the generality principle enhances the efficiency of the law is quite different from saying that the generality principle in law tends to promote the achievement of economic efficiency, defined as in conventional economic theory. Indeed, the opposing claim with respect to the second argument may seem more reasonable. Generality or equality before the law may reduce rather than enhance the relative achievement of orthodox efficiency norms, especially on some presupposition of economically sophisticated jurists who might, absent the generality constraints, direct resources to relatively more productive uses.

The claim here that the incorporation of the generality principle makes for a more efficient law is limited to the institutions of legal structure; the claim has no specific spillover relevance for resource usage beyond this structure itself. By more efficient law here, we refer only to those properties of generality that facilitate the operation and administration of law itself. Clearly, a recognized standard of equal treatment allows jurists to make decisions more quickly and with less arbitrariness. Further, decisions are more predictable – a quality that, in turn, reduces investment of legal resources in information concerning practices of particular jurists.

To a considerable extent, the administration of law must be decentralized. Law exerts its effect through litigation between and among private parties, and many jurists are confronted with the opposing claims of identified litigants in separate cases. The principle of generality is the basis for *stare decisis* – the practice that allows jurists to reach decisions by reference to like cases confronted by other jurists over a long course of recorded legal history. Absent some version of generality, the central role of precedence in legal practice would be reduced to insignificance. The coherence that precedence offers to the workings of the decentralized, but interlinked, legal nexus would be lost. Almost by necessity, a legal order without some variant of the generality principle would become more centralized, with separate jurists hierarchically tiered in some attempted furtherance of those standards that would be established in lieu of the equality norm. The self-organizing features of existing legal structures that do embody the generality precept to a large extent would be lost, with major implications for overall efficacy in legal procedures.[3]

E. Law and social purpose

The sometimes hackneyed term *law and order* conveys, at least indirectly, the distinctive feature of law that makes the generalization norm more readily acceptable than might seem to be the case with politics. Law, as traditionally understood, provides a framework within which persons carry on their own separate private purposes. Laws establish and enforce the boundaries or limits on admissible behavior. The law, as such, is presumed to have as its primary purpose the facilitation of personal interaction. In this conception, there is no social purpose to the law. Law, as administered and enforced by agents of the state, is not specifically designed to further explicitly defined social goals, whether these be maximization of economic value, full employment of the labor force, distributive justice, or harmony among organized interest groups.

Given the social purposelessness of law, as understood in this sense, the principle of equality under law (often referred to as *the rule of law*) emerges more or less naturally from considerations of both contractarian justice and efficiency. In this context, game metaphors are helpful. Law defines the rules of the social game, and elementary notions of fairness dictate that the same rules apply to all players. But note, in particular, that the generality norm here is itself defined as an attribute of fairness only because it reflects contractarian agreement. "Equality under law" – this standard is not drawn down from some externally ordered list of social purposes (or external standards of fairness) – a list that is presumed to exist independently of the preferences of the players or participants in the game itself.

If such an externally ordered list of social purposes should exist, equality under law might still survive as one among other social goals. But this principle in law would then be subject to possible trumping by other purposes that might be assigned priority. In this alternative scheme of things, the rule of law, as embodied in the generality precept, loses its pride of place. The principle cannot claim to remain the *sine qua non* of law itself.

It is interesting to observe that the generality principle has, in fact, survived despite the jurisprudential storms of the twentieth century. There have been frequent charges that law has been politicized, that modern jurists have overstepped traditional boundaries. This alleged politicization of law has, however, not often involved explicit departure from the rule of law as such in furtherance of social purpose. Instead, the politicization charges are levied against jurists who extend the range for the applicability of law beyond politically proscribed limits. That is to say, jurists are accused of usurping the role of political decision makers by making changes in law rather than enforcing law that exists while remaining within the constraints imposed by generality norms. This judicial overreaching may, of course, be motivated by social purposes. But jurists seemed to have remained reluctant to allow social purpose to subvert the constraints of generality directly, at least rhetorically. In civil rights cases, courts have often been willing to extend norms for equal treatment to interaction settings that have not, hitherto, been brought within previous interpretations of politically enacted statutes. Courts have, however, only rarely been willing to use overriding social purpose as an argument for providing support for unequal legal treatment.

F. Toward generality in politics

The widespread adherence, both in rhetoric and in reality, to the generality principle in law offers a basis for the extension of a comparable principle to politics. Equality under law informs public understanding in Western cultures. Violations of the equality norm invoke expressions of demonstrated unfairness accompanied by varying degrees of protest. Why, then, do citizens in Western democracies at the same time acquiesce in a politics that does not embody a comparable generality norm? Why is politics allowed to discriminate overtly among separate persons and groups and without protest when law is held to nondiscriminatory standards?

These and like questions find answers in two of the features that have already been discussed in earlier parts of this chapter. Politics has been considered to be different from law because it is assigned social purpose on varying interpretations of the whole enterprise. And politics is understood by many (theorists, analysts, and practitioners alike) to be a discovery process aimed at finding the good and the true for the polity treated as some organic unit, with a tenuous relationship, at best, to expressed preferences of citizens–participants. In this conceptual interpretation of political enterprise, it would indeed be difficult to mount persuasive argument in support of the generality precept in the abstract. But explicit rejection of this interpretation–understanding is itself central to the modern contractarian construction. In the contractarian foundations for the derivation of legitimate political coercion, there is and can be no overriding social purpose apart from that which might represent and reflect values that are shared by ultimate participants in the process – values that originate only with participants and that are so understood.

For precisely the same reasons applicable to law, a politics that fails to satisfy some variant of the generality–equality norm cannot be deemed to be legitimate. Such a discriminatory politics cannot pass the contractarian test. In reflective equilibrium and behind a veil of ignorance/uncertainty, persons could never agree to the establishment of political institutions that are predicted to discriminate explicitly in their operation. The politics of discrimination would not meet the agreement criterion that defines fairness or justice. And, also importantly, such a politics would necessarily be inefficient in a resource-wasting sense.

Persons who acknowledge the social purposelessness of law may, at the same time, challenge the extension to politics. They may be unwilling to agree that politics has no "social purpose" and that politics is best understood to offer, analogous to law, a parametric framework within which persons may act to advance *their own* purposes, whatever these may be. But how can social purpose be attributed to a polity apart from some abandonment of the precept that values emerge only from individual members? And if social values do exist separately, there is little basis for democracy itself to have independent normative significance.

In the conceptualization upon which our analysis rests, politics becomes the setting for *collective action* in which persons consider it privately advantageous to undertake actions to further shared, but still distinguishable, interests. In this sense, politics, like law, is above and beyond the particularized interests that individuals may seek within the parametric limits. No definition of these interests, whether separately or jointly pursued, is needed, and, indeed, none is even possible at the level of ultimate constitutional evaluation.

As subsequent discussion in this book suggests, the most difficult issue confronted in the whole analysis involves the normative argument in support of generality at the level of postconstitutional politics. Why must the generality precept be invoked in withdrawing normative support for political action that discriminates among separate groups of citizens? Might not *some* discrimination pass muster even under some idealized veil-of-ignorance construction? The response to this question introduces the necessary recognition that postconstitutional politics does not, itself, mirror, even conceptually, the unanimitarian idealization of the veil-of-ignorance construction. As it operates, postconstitutional politics is majoritarian, which is, naturally, discriminatory to the extent that participants promote separable interests. Recognizing this feature, veil-situated agreement would never be reached on the authorization of explicitly discriminatory political action at postconstitutional levels.

The remaining chapters in this book flesh out and elaborate the propositions. The treatment ranges from highly abstract models that may seem a long distance from grubby political reality all the way to practical issues of current policy.

Modern democratic politics is not working well. Few will challenge this basic diagnosis. But until and unless we recognize that the distributional politics that we observe is necessarily discriminatory and that this politics may be described in terms analogous to a Hobbesian "warre" of each interest against all others – a warre in which no one's interest is advanced – all efforts at putative reform must fail. Politics must be brought within the constraints defined by norms that can guarantee discussion and argument over general alternatives for collective–political choice.

PART TWO
Analysis

2 Majoritarian democracy

In reality, democratic politics is complex. We participate, directly or passively, in politics that we also observe, read about, and watch on our television screens. We confront an intricate and interlinked institutional jumble involving elections, candidates, referenda, parties, legislative bodies, executives, administrators, bureaucrats, regulations, decrees, mandates, program benefits, transfer payments, taxes, traditions, conventions, practices, and, of course, seemingly endless talk, almost always with a robust rhetoric of "public interest." We tend to be overwhelmed by politics, as if it is too much with us, late and soon. Perhaps it is as well that we should be because politics controls almost half of the aggregate allocation of economic value in the United States and more than one-half in the welfare states of Europe.

The complexity of politics makes analysis aimed at genuine understanding difficult to commence. It is almost as if we ask the question: How do we analyze "the world?" The task of understanding must be tackled in small steps, in bits and pieces, and undertaken by those who specialize in separate scientific disciplines. By necessity, the enterprise is analogous to the fable in which several blind men feel the elephant with each one subsequently trying to understand the whole animal.

Historians try to identify major events in the political record, and they seek to discover causal forces, both human and nonhuman, that help us explain those events. Political scientists examine the formal and informal institutional structures of politics, and they try to understand the actual functioning of these structures. Public-choice economists are more individualistic in their methods. They employ the economists' behavioral models in efforts to explain how alternative political institutions generate patterns of results. But all of these efforts, and others, fail, separately and jointly, to provide an understanding of democratic politics that is sufficiently comprehensive to allow for anything more than bases for piecemeal reform.

The situation demands heroic abstraction. It is essential that politics be analyzed first as "the forest" rather than as "the trees" that are the separate component elements. To take this step we must venture into what modern philosophers refer to as *ideal theory*, which may seem to bear little or no relationship to any underlying reality that is amenable to direct observation.

Any ideal theory of politics must incorporate both stylized positive analyses of what politics is really about and normative analyses of what politics should be about, if for no other reason than that politics must be, in part, influenced by what the participants in political order understand their own politics to be. In this chapter, we shall first sketch out what an ideal theory of politics would look like from a contractarian perspective – that which reflects our own normative interpretation and understanding. We then proceed to compare and contrast this theory with a stylized theory of that which we observe in the workings of modern majoritarian democracies. Critical analysis of majoritarianism, as viewed from the contractarian perspective, provides

is book. Genuine political reform must accomplish some
what majoritarian democracy is, along with some practical
reinterpretation through explicit constitutional change.

foundations: Politics as exchange

...ᴜ ᴜifficult to delineate the structural elements of an idealized politics
...ıᴛ ıs to articulate an abstract model of the workings of politics as observed. The
positive scientist can carry on the second task in either conscious or unconscious
disregard for possible incongruities between that which is and that which ought to
be. Whoever undertakes the first task, by contrast, must engage directly in normative
discourse, at least of a sort. What should an idealized politics do in a community
described by adherence to traditional liberal values, including the exclusive location
of evaluation in the consciousness of those who are participants? The moral or social
philosopher who would assay an answer is out of bounds if any external source of
evaluation is introduced or if any individual's preferences, including his or her own,
are elevated to a differentially influential criterial role. These constraints ensure that
idealized politics must remain substantively empty of specific content. Nonetheless,
necessary and sufficient procedural conditions may be defined – conditions that relate
specific results, whatever these may be, to the expressed values of the persons who
participate.

If the sources for evaluation are located only in the consciousness of persons, and
are known only by persons themselves, any moral legitimacy of coercion must be
derived ultimately from voluntary consent, whether actually or tacitly given. The
direct implication of normative individualism, as a philosophical starting point, is
that the idealized politics must reflect contractarian foundations. In summary terms,
"politics as exchange" becomes appropriately descriptive. Idealized politics becomes
an extension of the reciprocal and voluntary exchange processes of the market.

It is useful to examine the features of politics as exchange in some detail. Who is
exchanging with whom? And what is being exchanged? In its most abstract sense,
politics becomes the complex exchange among all members of a potential political
order, who personally and separately enter into the relationship because of shared
expectations of mutual gains. In this feature, political exchange is no different from
market exchange, except for the number of direct participants. That which is obtained
from political or collective action is some "good" that is commonly shared among all
participants (e.g., public order, education, and external defense), but the exchange, as
such, takes place among participants (beneficiaries), each one of whom "gives up"
(through taxes or other constraints on personal behavior) some share of the value
required to produce–supply that which is commonly demanded. And shares in this
value may be separately allocated. As with ordinary market exchange, agreement
among participants both specifies the terms of the contract and signals finalization of
the separate choices.

Note that these conditions for collective or political action remain procedural in
that they do not include definition or specification of what good is to be politically
provided or in what quantity. Agreement among all parties to the complex exchange

is the criterion for the efficiency of the interaction. There is no requirement that the terms of the exchange be defined independently of the process itself.

So much for a bare-bones summary of what are the elements of idealized politics within the contractarian perspective. But such a summary description masks a major difficulty. Precisely because the exchange that any idealized politics reflects is complex, in that all (*n*) participants must simultaneously enter into each trade or exchange, the attainment of agreement becomes more problematic because each party must engage in bargains with every other party. (This feature stands in dramatic contrast to market exchange in privately partitionable goods, in which only two parties engage, one with another.) In many-person trades, the costs of reaching agreement among all parties may be such as to make consummation of exchange contracts impossible.

The practicable difficulties of implementing any such idealized politics as exchange must, of course, be acknowledged. But such acknowledgment does not, in any way, remove the normative significance of the unanimity benchmark. As Knut Wicksell (1896) noted a century ago, any collective action worth its costs, as evaluated autonomously by participants, must be able, at least in principle, to command unanimous consent for its implementation at some cost-sharing arrangement. And, of course, for any collective action project that promises to yield a net surplus, there may exist many possible cost-sharing schemes. Recognition of the differential distributional gains from implementation of the action provides the motivation for separate bargaining strategies that may make ultimate agreement difficult to secure. Participants may find it privately rational to invest in strategy aimed at decreasing cost shares while they may acknowledge the mutuality of gain that agreement might make possible.

At this juncture, the ideal theory of politics as exchange may seem to offer little or no understanding or guidance for the institutional realities of collective action. The unanimity requirement may be dismissed, even as a benchmark criterion, once the difficulties of reaching agreement on the distribution of cost shares are fully acknowledged. And, even if these difficulties are deemed somehow surmountable, in some idealized sense, for collective action aimed at supplying commonly shared goods, they emerge in exacerbated form when welfare transfers are considered.

How, then, might the contractarian enterprise be rescued?

A central contribution of *The Calculus of Consent* (Buchanan and Tullock, 1962) involved a proffered answer. The Wicksellian criterion of unanimity may be shifted "upward" to the stage or level of choices among rules (constitutions). This step serves two analytical purposes. First, it eliminates the unanimity requirement for agreement on particularized within-period political choices, thereby substantially reducing the personal motivation for bargaining over differential shares in distributional gains. As Wicksell recognized, any relaxation of the unanimity constraint dramatically modifies the strategic environment; a single player or participant no longer occupies a potential holdout position vis-à-vis all others. Second, and related, application of the unanimity norm at the constitutional level of choices among rules acts to reduce the potential for distributional conflict by the necessary introduction of uncertainty concerning the impact of alternative rules on identified interests of persons and groups. By necessity, a choice among rules that are to remain in place over a series of periods, during which many within-rule choices are to be made, creates a veil of uncertainty that makes explicit distributional motivation less likely to emerge. Hence, bargaining over rules is more likely to be analogous to scientific disputation over the working properties of alternatives; disputes will tend to center around theories and away from interests (Vanberg and Buchanan, 1989).

The shift of the Wicksellian benchmark norm to the level of constitutional politics allows the contractarian perspective of politics as exchange to be retained while, either conceptually or empirically, ordinary political actions may take place in the clear absence of consensus. The inclusive "game of politics," considered as a continuing interaction over many periods, in each of which many separate political actions may be carried out, may remain potentially positive sum for all participants. That is to say, persons may be considered to have agreed (or might have agreed) upon the basic rules, even in the anticipation that, on particular occasions, their own interests would be damaged by political action. This stance would depend critically on the prediction that, over the whole set of political actions that might be taken under the operation of chosen rules, benefits would exceed costs.

In popular as well as professional discourse, democratic politics is associated directly with majority rule. What role does majority rule play in the inclusive contractarian interpretation and understanding? As was emphasized in *The Calculus of Consent*, there is nothing either theoretically unique or morally sacrosanct about the majority decision rule, as such. Within the generalized contractarian model, however, majority rule may emerge as an important, perhaps the dominant, means through which political choices at the within-constitutional level are made. This is to say, there is no necessary inconsistency between majority rule, in period, and the inclusive politics as exchange paradigm, provided that certain side conditions are met. These conditions may be summarized in the statement that the sequential political game played within majority rule must be positive sum both in the aggregate and for each player separately. These conditions do not rule out discrete political action in which some persons and groups gain while others lose. What the conditions do rule out are payoffs that are sensed to be negative by any participant or group of participants over the whole set of anticipated political choices, the base point being defined by positions achieved when the majority rule, collective action game is not played at all.

B. Contract breached: Politics as taking

As suggested earlier, the normative stance that exclusively locates the sources for evaluation in individuals leads, necessarily in our view, to some sort of contractarian exercise of legitimization or justification for politics. The contrasting vision in which external sources of evaluation are presumed to exist may, of course, incorporate a rejection of the whole contractarian enterprise. In any such vision, ordinary persons are no longer the ultimate sovereigns but are, instead, subject to the value standards dictated by those individuals or institutions that claim access to fonts of revealed or discovered truth. As noted, elements of this theory of politics remain with us in both everyday and scholarly discourse, but we do not propose to criticize this alternative vision further.

Our concern in this section is to examine the understanding of politics that does not evoke external value norms or standards but that, at the same time, categorically rejects the contractarian effort to establish putative legitimacy. In this alternative model, politics becomes, quite straightforwardly, an arena of conflict, in which members of dominating coalitions take desired goods from those who are outside the memberships. Hence, our subtitle for this section, "Politics as Taking." Politics, here, is essentially distributional. The Hobbesian warre is simply transferred to the realm of institutionally organized conflict. Or, to adapt Marxian terminology, politics is a continuation of war by other means, or vice versa.

In this conception of the political enterprise, there can be no normatively grounded limits on what can be done. Ultimate legitimization may be sought in some alleged correspondence between what is done and the "will of the people" generally, as was claimed by Communist regimes, or in democracy, which has come to be equated with majority electoral-decision processes in non-Communist settings. In the latter view, so long as political actions are determined by majoritarian coalitions, there are no grounds for complaint or concern on behalf of those persons or groups that may be differentially exploited. There is, indeed, no constitutionally protected sphere of activity into which politics cannot potentially enter. In essence, majoritarian agreement is the ultimate source of value. All and everything are politicizable.

When stated this baldly, many who might accept the democracy model may draw back and acknowledge, albeit reluctantly, the usefulness of a limited contractarian construction. Majority rule may be accepted as the *sine qua non* of democratic politics, but majority rule, standing alone, cannot offer guarantees of permanence of the rule itself. Majority coalitions, once in authority, might well act to eliminate electoral processes, thereby ensuring permanence in office. In recognition of this, and similar dangers, those who consider themselves to be strict majoritarians may, at the same time, become constitutionalists of sorts in their support for enforceable guarantees of electoral succession and open voting franchise. Such constitutionalism must, however, be "extramajoritarian" and may best be derived from some contractarian logic of consensus.

This "constitutional majoritarianism" is the conception of democratic politics that we propose to use to be descriptive of the most widely held modern attitude in Western politics. So long as the voting franchise is universal, elections are periodic, majority or plurality rules determine electoral winners, and legislative bodies operate with internal majority rules, there are no limits on the range and scope for political action.

Note, in particular, that in this model, politics may be purely distributional. Majority coalitions may authorize the taking of economic value (measured by claims to assets and income flows) for any declared "public" purpose, including direct payments to designated groups. Our section's subtitle might be expanded to "Politics as Taking and Giving."

It is perhaps clear that the public acceptability of this majoritarian model of politics depends critically on some implicit presumption that electoral, and hence parliamentary, majorities are not permanent. If a dominant majority coalition could ensure its own continuance in authority, once empowered, it would seem difficult to advance an intellectually respectable argument for democracy. In the implicit understanding here, dominant coalitions rotate sequentially over electoral periods, not necessarily on a regular or predictable cycle, but, nonetheless, with sufficient frequency (at least expectationally) to ensure some modicum of generalized representation of all interests. (Two examples from the 1990s suggest that modern democracies approach crises when this rotational feature is sensed to be missing. Italy's constitutional revolution of 1993 and 1994 stemmed, in part, from general public awareness that the effective ruling coalition had secured permanence in office. A somewhat less dramatic shift in public attitudes was observed in 1994 in the United States with the enhanced awareness of long-standing one-party domination of the Congress.)

In this book, our analysis is not based on any diagnosis of democracy's "failure." Indeed, quite the opposite. We use as our benchmark the idealized majoritarian process – a political structure in which there remain constitutional guarantees of universal franchise, periodic elections, and majority rule within legislatures. Further, we presume that historical forces, along with individual preferences, ensure that there is rotation among ruling coalitions. Our criticism is directed at this model, but with a difference. We do not propose, in this book, to outline a structure for politics that would emerge from an idealized contractarian–constitutional perspective. (This effort has occupied us elsewhere.) Our current purpose is more limited. We take majoritarianism, as previously described, to be the central criterion in the existing understanding of democracy, which we also presume to occupy a place in individual values. Specifically, we shall examine the prospects for procedural rather than subject-matter limits on "Politics as Taking."

C. The objects for political choice

Choices are what the activity of politics is all about. Political choices are often distinguished from economic choices by the mutual exclusiveness of alternatives, once chosen. Or, in terms more familiar to economists, political choices tend to be of the "either-or" variety, whereas economic choices tend to be "more or less." This distinction will be relevant to some of the discussion to follow. But, first, we want to examine the nature of the alternatives for political choice, as these are implicitly perceived to exist in accepted public and scientific understanding of majoritarian democracy. In the next section, we challenge this general understanding, and we shall discuss some implications from a differing perspective, thereby introducing some of the arguments to be developed later in the book.

In the most abstract sense, political choices are made among discrete "social states" – a term that is widely used in formal social choice theory or among sets of possible social states. Rigorously defined, a social state is a vector that fully specifies the position of each and every person in the relevant community.[1] Clearly, a social state, so defined, is unique, and the presence of any defined state necessarily precludes the simultaneous existence of any other state, or of any elements thereof. It follows, definitionally, that social states may be considered "public goods" in the full Samuelsonian sense (Samuelson, 1954). That is to say, a social state, if present for one person in the polity, must be present for all other persons.

By saying that the alternatives for political choice are social states, we are not suggesting that all or even a large number of the many-faceted vector become variables in any relevant subset of alternatives faced by the collectivity. Here, as elsewhere, the mathematics of partial derivation are helpful, both analytically and practicably. A political choice may be reduced to one between two members of a subset, hence, a pairwise selection between options that differ, one from another, in only one component of the vector that describes the complete social state. This dimensionality aspect of political choice need not concern us here, nor has this aspect been central to scientific analysis over the half century. What has occupied the attention of social choice theorists, almost exclusively, is the failure of majoritarian decision processes to generate stability in outcomes when more than two alternatives are in the relevant subset. The logical possibility of majoritarian cycles, under nonrestricted preference domains, brought into modern scientific discussion by Arrow (1951) and Black (1958), has stimulated intensive efforts to circumvent the stark implications of the basic instability result.

We propose to start with the cyclical feature of majoritarian decision processes and to acknowledge that, in the absence of constitutional constraints on the domain of alternatives, the presence of this feature may be necessary to make majoritarianism acceptable to those who are subject to its dictates. As one of us noted more than four decades ago (Buchanan, 1954), an unconstrained political setting in which majoritarian results remain stable ensures only the permanent exploitation of a well-identified minority.

D. The endogeneity of alternatives

Commence, therefore, with a setting in which any and all majoritarian outcomes (generated by the relevant coalitions of persons) are acknowledged to be unstable and vulnerable to displacement by some other alternative when presented in the appropriate phase of the electoral cycle. We assume that there are no restrictions on the domain of alternatives. We want to examine more carefully the characteristics of the alternatives that may emerge. And we consider this problem as an expectational one that might be faced by an individual either as a potential member of an existing majority coalition or of a minority that might have prospects for achieving majority status.

What is the makeup of the subset of alternatives likely to be considered for political choice? This subset will depend, in part, on the rule under which choices are to be made. That is to say, the subset of alternatives from among which choice is to be made is endogenous to the operation of the decision rule, rather than exogenous, as has been almost universally presumed in social and public-choice analysis. The subset of alternatives for majoritarian choice is itself determined by the fact that majority rule is operative. Note that the endogeneity here is not equivalent to agenda control, which has been exhaustively analyzed. The theory of agenda control embodies the presumption that the set of alternatives from which a selection is to be made exists independently of the rule; agenda manipulation involves the ordering of the alternatives within this set.

As social states, all conceivably feasible alternatives must exist as potentialities. But only a specific subset assumes pride of place for explicit consideration when the decision rule is specified. This endogeneity feature has the effect of dramatically reducing the size of the subset of options over which majority rule is allowed to operate. Choice options that are dominated in payoffs for members of the dominant majority coalition will not be considered; these options will simply not be eligible.[2] It follows that outcomes or solutions to the majoritarian game cannot be symmetrical in payoffs over all participants. Options with this characteristic feature would never be placed on the agenda by the coalition that achieves dominance. Relevant alternatives must, therefore, embody asymmetry in payoffs, as between members of the majority and persons outside this coalition. In this sense, majority rule can never be nondistributional. And a choice alternative that might be classified as nondistributional, for example, a Samuelsonian public good (Samuelson, 1954) financed by Lindahl taxes (Lindahl, 1919), will always be dominated for members of a majority by an alternative solution; for example, one that might involve the same good in the same quantity financed by imposing tax prices on the persons outside the majority coalition that are higher than those defined by Lindahl criteria.

E. Simplified illustration

In this section, we present the ideas developed earlier in the simplest possible setting. Consider the position of a person (*A*) who is a member of a potential majority coalition. Suppose that the anticipated payoff from failure to take specific political action is set at zero, as shown in Cell IV, Figure 2.1. The first number measures the ordinal payoff to a member of *A*, the second, the payoff to a nonmember of the majority coalition. The majority is empowered to choose among possible social states, each of which defines payoffs to *all* members of the polity.

Suppose, now, that political action might be taken that yields symmetrical payoffs to members of *A* and all others in the polity (*B*). That is, Cell I, Figure 2.1, is a possible political result, where payoffs are positive at 1 for each participant.

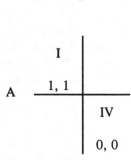

Figure 2.1. No conflict.

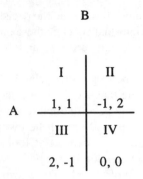

Figure 2.2. Differential advantage.

Will *A*, along with others in the majority coalition, allow the option represented in the Cell I set of payoffs to be realized? The answer is positive if the social states described in Cells I and IV are the only ones that are possible. The answer is negative, however, if there exist other options available that dominate the Cell I payoffs for members of the majority. See Figure 2.2. If Cell III is an available choice option, the majority coalition that includes *A* will impose this alternative to the no-action status quo (Cell IV). The political choice that generates the symmetrical payoff result (Cell I) will never be the outcome of majoritarian choice.

The point to be emphasized is that the set of options that might be potentially selected under the operation of majority rule does not exist independently of this rule. To demonstrate this point, consider the simplest possible comparison – that between the operation of a unanimity rule and a majority rule. Under the unanimity rule, the action that produces the symmetrical payoff in Cell I becomes the only alternative to the Cell IV status quo, and because the payoffs in Cell I dominate those in Cell IV for all participants, it will emerge. With the majority rule operative, however, this action is precluded by the dominance of the Cell III outcome, for members of the majority that includes *A*.

It is straightforward to fill in the payoffs in Cell II, so as to reflect the results anticipated by *A* when the majority that includes *A* is replaced by the majority that now includes *B*, where symmetry in ordinal rankings is assumed.

The four-cell payoff matrix in Figure 2.2 looks like that of the classical prisoners' dilemma (PD). We note here, however, that the interaction discussed is not that of the PD and that there are quite different behavioral implications. The critical difference lies in the fact that, here, there is only one choice alternative to be selected, regardless of the rule through which this choice is made. By contrast, in the PD setting, or in any genuine game, each player confronts separate choice options, and an outcome emerges as a consequence of the interactive meshing of the separately made choices. In the simple matrix illustration, Player *A* chooses between rows, Player *B* chooses between columns. An outcome emerges from a combined row–column set of choices. The outcome, as such, is not explicitly chosen. In the political choice model analyzed here, by contrast, cells of the matrix (outcomes) can be chosen, and the decision rule determines the relevant set of such alternatives. Actions that generate these outcomes are specifically chosen; the outcomes, as such, do not emerge from separately chosen strategies on the part of two or more players.

The difference here may be critically important for behavior. In the classical PD, as experiments have shown, players who anticipate more than single or one-shot plays will tend to behave more cooperatively than the simple payoff structure would suggest. In the political choice setting analyzed here, it is as if one of the two players should be allowed, unilaterally, to choose among the standard set of four cells in each period, with the choice authority being somehow randomly rotated between the two players, period by period, over a whole sequence of periods. The player who is assigned choice authority in any period will be less likely to behave cooperatively (i.e., choose the action that generates the symmetrical set of payoffs), even in anticipation of the continuing sequence of plays, than would be the case in the comparable PD setting. In situations in which newly emergent majorities are formed and secure majoritarian dominance by attracting members from old majority coalitions is shown, the behavioral impact of anticipated coalitional rotation seems likely to be negligible, so long as the rules are taken as given. Majorities that are in positions of choice authority will almost surely act so as to maximize payoffs to their own members.

F. Need politics be positive sum?

As the illustrative examples suggest, majoritarian politics is not properly classified as a game in the sense that outcomes or solutions are not determined by the emergent result of separated choices of players. By comparison, in majoritarian politics outcomes that define the actions of all persons are chosen by defined coalitions. Outcomes do not emerge in consequence of a set of interactive strategies. The game analogy remains, nonetheless, helpful when we look at the implications for stability and viability. In an ordinary game, or in politics modeled as exchange, there are at least indirect guarantees that all participants expect to secure net benefits from being in the game, or at least do not expect to suffer net damage. In ordinary games, players are presumed to have exit options available; at some cost, they can simply walk away, which they would be expected to do if the expected payoffs should remain negative over the appropriately defined sequence of plays. If politics is considered in some ultimate sense to be based on a contractual consensus, at least as stylized, legitimacy is undermined if particular individuals or classes of individuals face expected losses from the whole enterprise.

With politics as taking, however, legitimacy does not depend on consent, even at some constitutional level, and, as noted earlier, the analogue is really that of institutionally structured war among potential coalitions. There are no necessary protections or guarantees against political actions that generate harmful results to particular persons in specific electoral periods, and, as coalitions rotate, all participants may possibly be damaged, in net, by political action. That is to say, even if periodicity in elections ensures against permanence in office, there is nothing in majoritarian politics that acts to make benefit cost-ratios positive, either for specific-period actions or for a whole

B

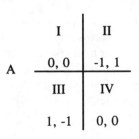

Figure 2.3. No mutual gain.

B

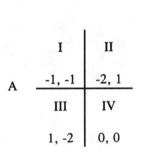

Figure 2.4. Mutual damage with differential advantage.

sequence. To the extent that all participants lose, in net, there will be, of course, a basis for constitutional change that will restrict majoritary exploitation. But romantic ideas about democracy may make such change difficult to implement.

Once again, a simple numerical illustration may be useful. Consider, in Figure 2.3, a variant of the matrix in Figure 2.2. Suppose, now, that there is no action that could be mutually beneficial to all participants; there is no set of payoffs in some analogue to Cell I that dominates the status quo set in Cell IV. For a potential majority coalition, however, whether it be that represented by *A* or *B* as a member, the absence of a symmetrical payoff set with positively valued entries does not ensure inaction. An *A* majority may choose political action that imposes a net cost on members of the minority while offering net benefits to members of the majority.

If coercive exactions from members of a minority and payments to members of a majority can be made without excess burdens, the political game is, of course, zero sum, as the numbers in Figure 2.3 indicate. If, however, as either the logic of analysis or empirical evidence suggests, excess burdens of transfers are present, the strictly redistributional operations of majoritarian politics are clearly negative sum.

Or, consider the illustration in Figure 2.4, in which symmetry or generality in treatment as between members of majority and minority coalitions would be mutually damaging. Differentially positive payoffs to successful majorities may remain as prospects, however, and, if the activity is politicized, all persons suffer utility losses over the whole sequence of periods.

The important point to be emphasized is that majoritarian politics, in itself, creates alternatives for political choice and actions that necessarily include distributional elements, quite apart from the possible existence or nonexistence of collective alternatives that are positive sum in some aggregative sense. From the recognition of this point there follows the implication that, in many situations, the redistributional alternatives may come to dominate those that might yield larger benefits in some aggregate measure (Flowers and Danzon, 1984).

3   Eliminating the off diagonals

The highly stylized and abstract models of small-number interactions introduced at the end of Chapter 2 suggest the possible efficacy of constitutional constraints in reducing the size of the set of outcomes attainable under majority voting rules. By appropriate definition of the dimensions that describe the vector of outputs under collective action, the distinction between positions on and off the diagonals in the simple matrix illustrations facilitates precision in the classification of positions in accordance with the generality principle. In the stylized models to be used further throughout the book, positions on the matrix diagonals embody symmetry or generality in the collectively imposed behavioral adjustments among the interacting parties; positions off the diagonal embody asymmetry or differential adjustments along the separate dimensions, thereby a violation of the generality criterion.

Section A relates the matrix construction to the more familiar analyses of majority voting in conventional public choice theory. In Section B we extend the model to three parties, and we specify more carefully the elements of the matrix construction. In the process we clarify the meaning of the distinction made between solutions on and off the diagonals. In this section we assume that all participants are identical in the sense that the public good is equally productive for all and that the supply of inputs to produce this good is equally costly. In Section C we examine the incentives for rent seeking under unconstrained and constrained majority rule. In Section D we drop the assumption of identical evaluation. Section E discusses the effect of the on-diagonal constraint on majority stability. Section F introduces the concept of political efficiency more generally, which we compare with the more familiar notion of economic efficiency.

A. The necessity of majoritarian cycles

Return to the simple matrix construction introduced earlier as Figure 2.2, reproduced here as Figure 3.1.

Note precisely what this apparently innocent construction implies for the operation of majority rule politics. Recall that A is identified as one member, or the representative member, of a coalition that may be assigned decisive control over collective action, which amounts to the selection of one of the four possible social states depicted in the matrix. B is identified analogously as one member of a different coalition that might, alternatively, be assigned control. One or the other of the two coalitions is assumed to be decisive.

The social state chosen as the outcome for the inclusive group is different when the locus of authority shifts. The A coalition selects the outcome in Cell III, with the indicated set of payoffs, whereas the B coalition, when and if it becomes decisive, selects the outcome in Cell II. There is a rotation in collective action as the controlling

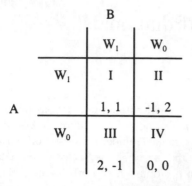

Figure 3.1. Rotating majority coalitions.

majority changes. There is no social state that remains stable in the face of shifting majorities.

The relationship between the stylized construction here and the familiar setting for the analyses of majority voting deserves attention. In the latter, the focus of inquiry is on the prospect for instability in the operation of majority rule as separate alternatives are presented in a series of pairwise choices. The early public-choice analysis showed that, by restricting collective choices to alternatives arrayed along a single dimension, with all other components of the vector defining a social state parametrically fixed, stable majority outcomes may emerge under certain narrowly restricted configurations of individual preferences. This model is, of course, the base from which median voter theorems arise, incorporating the single peakedness of preference orderings over the alternatives. If the dimensionality of the choice set is expanded, the standard analysis shows that majority cycles will occur under almost any and all configurations of preferences.

As indicated earlier and also in Chapter 2, at least in the stylized model, prospective majority coalitions will always select an alternative that will embody distributional advantages to its members. The restrictive conditions required to produce even the possibility of single peakedness will be violated, intentionally and deliberately, by the members of the prospective winning majority coalition in order to gain distributional advantage. If this point is acknowledged, the implication is that majority voting processes necessarily generate cycles so long as sequential voting choices are guaranteed to occur, and so long as the makeup of coalitions is allowed to shift over these choices.

Note that the model stylized here is not one in which voters are presented with exogenously chosen comparisons among alternatives. The alternatives are themselves selected, and chosen, over some existing status quo, because a majority coalition is organized in support, and because the prospectively selected alternative embodies promised distributional advantage to members. Individual preferences are not changed over the sequence of voting choices, and we follow standard procedure in assuming that each preference ordering exhibits the required properties to ensure rational choice.

B. Asymmetry in the off-diagonals

The discussion in Section A is a digression from our main argument, designed to forestall criticism from conventional public-choice theorists who might object that our stylized construction models rotation among majority coalitions somewhat too cavalierly. As the matrix construction suggests, the four possible elements in the collective choice set may be described as incorporating two dimensions, indicated by the rows and columns. We may think of these separate dimensions as "the actions of *A*" (rows) and "the actions of *B*" (columns), as is familiar from game theoretic usage of similar models. A collective choice would, then, involve the dictation of specific courses of action for all parties to the interaction; the solution is multidimensional. But the construction remains essentially empty until the entries in the rows and columns are more fully identified. The four elements in the choice set, with the differing payoffs as indicated, might be reached by almost any combination of actions of the two parties.

For our purposes, the significant step involves the specification of symmetry in the actions of the two parties in some of the elements and its absence in others. Think of the row and column entries as inputs that might be provided by the separate persons toward the production of a good that is to be made available to all members of the community. By way of practical illustration, think of David Hume's classic example of neighboring farmers who live alongside a swampy meadow that needs draining. Each person may either work toward draining the meadow or not work. Think, simply, of a two-person interaction, but one that is employed here as an analogue for the many-person setting. The subscripts to the ws in the rows and columns describe the amount of work, say, in weeks per year, provided by each person.

Note that the ws are arrayed in such a fashion that symmetry between the actions of the parties characterizes all outcomes on the northwest–southeast diagonal. In each of these outcomes, each of the parties provides the same input to the production of the public good. By contrast, note that in each off-diagonal cell, differing inputs are provided by the two persons. In Cell II, for example, Individual *A* provides one week's work, whereas Individual *B* provides nothing. In Cell III, by comparison, Individual *B* provides one week's work, whereas Individual *A* does nothing. In all outcomes, the good, in whatever quantity that is produced, remains equally available to both parties.

In our extension of this simple construction to depict majoritarian politics, the majority coalition represented by *A* will impose the solution of Cell III, where its members will not contribute, or contribute differentially less, to the production of the commonly-used good than will those persons outside the coalition. And vice versa when the majority coalition shifts. As we have emphasized, the operation of majority voting, unless constrained, will tend to generate off-diagonal rather than diagonal solutions. Majority rule, in itself, tends to ensure that the principle of generality is violated.

The construction suggests that majority rule may operate so as to generate solutions that are symmetrical in behavioral adjustments among dimensions only if there are explicit constraints put on the set of possible elements in the collective or political choice set. Effective reform in the rules must, somehow, eliminate off-diagonal solutions from being among those that might be selected by a majority coalition. Consider a constitutional rule that requires all collective actions to be characterized by symmetry in treatment among or in action by all parties in attaining the chosen outcome. In our elementary construction, this rule would require that the two parties provide the same amount of work toward producing the public good. In the two-row, two-column matrix illustration here, this rule would require that each person work either a week or not at all.

Note that, in this case, the solution shown in Cell I will emerge no matter which majority is decisive, and, further, note that the operation of majority rule will generate results equivalent to those that would be forthcoming under a rule of unanimity. These implications stem from the assumption of identity in preferences, which makes the collective decision rule irrelevant when genuine publicness is present, in all dimensions. This relationship can be illustrated by extending the model to three rather than two interacting parties, treated either as persons or as representatives of separate coalitions.

Three-person interaction. Consider Figure 3.2, and here it may be helpful, once again, to think of David Hume's meadow, this time with three neighboring farmers, each one of whom will find the productivity of his farm increased by draining the swamp, no matter who might contribute effort in the undertaking. Assume that there are four possible assignments for each farmer, to be settled in a collective decision; each may be assigned three weeks, two weeks, one week, or no work at all; these alternatives may be designated by w_3, w_2, w_1, and w_0, respectively.

We continue to assume that evaluations of the separate parties are identical. In order to present the analysis in the two dimensions of the page's surface, each of the sixteen cells in the four-by-four matrix describing the behavior of A and B must contain four sets of payoffs, one each for an action assigned to C, the third party to the interaction. The top row, in each of the sixteen cells, indicates the payoffs to all persons when C carries out, at collective orders, the w_3 action. The second row similarly corresponds to Cs undertaking the w_2 action, the third row for Cs w_1 action, and the bottom row within each cell emerges when C is assigned no action toward generating the common or public good.

For purposes of expositional simplicity, the payoffs may be treated as utility indicators that are intrapersonally comparable in the sense that ordinal rankings are invariant under increasing monotonic transformation. Under the assumption of identical preferences, any numerical representation of payoffs would, of course, be the same for all persons. The numerical payoffs in the matrix of Figure 3.2 are calculated on the assumption that inputs are supplied at a uniform rate (opportunities foregone in other value-producing activities) and that the productivity of the public good declines over quantity. (Details are provided at the bottom of the figure.) Note that there are sixty-four possible social states or imputations defined by the separate actions of each of the three parties.

Consider, first, the operation of unconstrained majority rule in the context of this simple three-person, public goods example. As a first step, we can eliminate certain solutions by a criterion of majority dominance (Buchanan 1996, 1997), introduced

		B			
		W$_3$	W$_2$	W$_1$	W$_0$
	W$_3$	I **9, 9, 9** 7, 7, 22 4, 4, 34 0, 0, 45	II 7, 22, 7 4, 19, 19 0, 15, 30 -5, 10, 40	III 4, 34, 4 0, 30, 15 -5, 25, 25 -11, 19, 34	IV 0, 45, 0 -5, 40, 10 -11, 34, 19 -18, 27, 27 *M*
	W$_2$	V 22, 7, 7 19, 4, 19 15, 0, 15 10, -5, 40	VI 19, 19, 4 **15, 15, 15** 10, 10, 25 4, 4, 34	VII 15, 30, 0 10, 25, 10 4, 19, 19 -3, 12, 27	VIII 10, 40, -5 4, 34, 4 -3, 27, 12 -11, 19, 19
A	W$_1$	IX 34, 4, 4 30, 0, 15 25, -5, 25 19, -11, 34	X 30, 15, 0 25, 10, 10 19, 4, 19 12, -3, 27	XI 25, 25, -5 19, 19, 4 **12, 12, 12** 4, 4, 19	XII 19, 34, -11 12, 27, -3 4, 19, 4 -5, 10, 10
	W$_0$	XIII 45, 0, 0 40, -5, 10 34, -11, 19 27, -18, 27 *M*	XIV 40, 10, -5 34, 4, 4 27, -3, 12 19, -11, 19	XV 34, 19, -11 27, 12, -3 19, 4, 4 10, -5, 10	XVI 27, 27, -18 *M* 19, 19, -11 10, 10, -5 **0, 0, 0**

Figure 3.2. Three person, public good illustration.

The payoffs are computed as follows:
(1) Each unit of input is supplied at a cost of 15 units of opportunity value, constant over quantities.
(2) Units of output, equally available to all persons, are measured one for one with units of input, with value product in accordance with the following schedule:

Units of output	Total Value Product (to each person)
1	10
2	19
3	27
4	34
5	40
6	45
7	49
8	52
9	54

previously in Chapter 2. No majority coalition, whether AB, AC, or BC, would propose a collective alternative that involves lower payoffs to both parties than other solutions available. For illustration, look at the imputation $(7, 7, 22)$ in Cell I, Row 2, which is generated if A and B each provides three units of input and C provides two units. Note that this solution is dominated in payoffs *for any majority*. For an AB coalition, for illustration, $(7, 7, 22)$ is dominated by, say, $(27, 27, -18)$ in Cell XVI, Row 1; for an AC coalition, with the two payoffs $(7, 22)$, the solution is dominated by $(27, -18, 27)$ Cell XIII, Row 4; for the BC coalition, $(7, 22)$ is majority dominated by $(-18, 27, 27)$ Cell IV, Row 4, along with many other alternatives in the set.

By the criterion of majority dominance, we can eliminate forty-six of the sixty-four possible solutions or outcomes. None of these would emerge under the operation of unconstrained majority rule because any of these solutions would be dominated in payoffs for *any* majority. The remaining positions or alternatives make up the set of alternatives that are nondominated for majority coalitions. These are shown in Figure 3.3. No change can be made, as between any two of the nondominated positions, without lowering payoffs (or leaving payoffs unchanged) to at least one person of some two-person majority coalition.

Note that the eighteen majority nondominated positions also make up the set of alternatives among which unconstrained majority voting will cycle, if it is presumed that these alternatives are presented in a series of pairwise comparisons. For illustration, suppose that the position depicted by the imputation $(40, 10, -5)$, Cell XIV, should be in place and opposed by $(-5, 40, 10)$, Cell IV. Clearly, the majority BC would approve the change. But $(-5, 40, 10)$ could then be defeated by $(10, -5, 40)$, Cell V, which could, in time, be defeated by $(40, 10, -5)$, the initial position. And, of course, the cycle need not be among the set of only the four payoff imputations used illustratively here. For example, $(40, 10, -5)$ is also majority dominated for the BC coalition by $(-11, 19, 34)$, Cell III, which is, in turn, majority dominated for AB by $(27, 27, -18)$, and so forth.

We can reduce the size of the set of likely outcomes of unconstrained majority rule if we impose a payoff symmetry condition among members of the majority. If we require that members of the two-person majority coalition share gains from imposed collective action symmetrically between themselves, we reduce the size of the majority set to the three imputations marked by the Ms in Figures 3.2 and 3.3. Note that, in each of these configurations, the person in the minority is maximally exploited. The property of symmetry adds an element of quasi-stability. Von Neumann and Morgenstern (1944) called the analogous set the *solution set* for the majority rule game. Clearly, solutions that embody, or even approximate, the embodiment of symmetry in sharing among majority coalition members are less vulnerable to displacement by shifting majority coalitions. Again, for illustration, suppose that the AB coalition forms and enforces the $(45, 0, 0)$ solution. Surely, this result, in which B's position is not improved at all by the collective action, is more vulnerable to change imposed by a new BC majority than would be the case with, say, the C $(34, 19, -11)$ solution.

Among the sixty-four possible imputations in the construction, there are only four in which all of the three parties in the interaction are treated symmetrically, as defined by the actions collectively assigned to each. These four on-diagonal imputations are shown in bold typeface in Figure 3.2. Note particularly, however, that *none* of these

B

		W₃	W₂	W₁	W₀
A	W₃	I 0, 0, 45	II -5, 10, 40	III -11, 19, 34	IV 0, 45, 0 -5, 40, 10 -11, 34, 19 -18, 27, 27 *M*
	W₂	V 10, -5, 40	VI	VII	VIII 10, 40, -5
	W₁	IX 19, -11, 34	X	XI	XII 19, 34, -11
	W₀	XIII 45, 0, 0 40, -5, 10 34, -11, 19 27, -18, 27 *M*	XIV 40, 10, -5	XV 34, 19, -11	XVI 27, 27, -18 *M*

Figure 3.3. Figure 3.2 with all majority-dominated imputations eliminated.

Note: The distinction between the set of all feasible alternatives and the subset here defined as majority nondominated depends, of course, on the parameters of the particular numerical example.

symmetrical solutions show up in the reduced set of nondominated positions shown in Figure 3.3. Each of these symmetrical results is majority dominated and could never emerge under the operaton of nonconstrained majority voting. Symmetry or generality among all parties emerges under majority rule only if the possible set of alternatives is constitutionally constrained. It is not surprising that, if the constitutional rules are such that solutions on the diagonal are the only alternatives open for consideration (four alternatives in the illustration), the three parties would agree in their ranking. Regardless of the decision rule, whether the collective decision is made by dictatorship, majority rule, or by unanimity, and whether the AB, AC, or BC majority coalition assumes decision authority, the result will be the assignment of w_2 to each of the three players, generating the (15, 15, 15) payoff imputation in Figure 3.2. This particular feature of the model stems, of course, from the assumption of identical evaluations.

C. Rent seeking and the off-diagonals

Why are solutions on rather than off diagonals more desirable in some constitutional sense?

Consider, first, the collective decision process when the choice set is constrained to incorporate symmetry or generality in the assignment of action to the separate parties. In this setting, no participant has an incentive to invest resources in efforts to secure differential or discriminatory advantage at the expense of others in the collective enterprise. Persons may, of course, make efforts to become more informed about the alternatives that are confronted, and they may also engage in both explicit and implicit dialogue with others before revealing an ordering in the choice process itself. But this behavior takes place in full knowledge that any outcome, as defined by the set of collectively imposed assignments, embodies symmetry among all participants. The individual who seeks information and who communicates with others is engaged in a search that may, quite properly, be said to be "in the public interest." For purposes of clarifying the exposition here, we shall refer to this benchmark setting as that in which no behavior motivated by discriminatory distributional advantage occurs.

Let us now return attention to the nonconstrained operation of majority rule while remaining within the confines of the model that assumes identity in evaluation. Refer, again, to the numerical example depicted in Figure 3.2. Consider the effects of the absence of constitutional constraints on investment by the several participants that is motivated by the prospects of securing political authority for discriminatory advantage. Note that the differential in payoffs between members of the majority coalition and those in the minority emerges exclusively because of the opportunities for differential or discriminatory treatment as between these two positions. Each and every one of the majority nondominated outcomes in Figure 3.3 embodies substantial differentiation in treatment as among members of the majority and the minority. It is now clearly worthwhile for a participant to be a member of the decisive coalition, and it will, therefore, be rational for any person to invest resources in trying to secure such membership. We should expect some investment in pure rent seeking to take place (Buchanan, 1995b). For each person, there is a positive expected value for majority coalition membership, although such value largely emerges exclusively at the expense of those whose rent-seeking efforts fail and who find themselves in the minority. Even in cases in which the result is a simple transfer of resources from the minority to the majority, investment in majoritarian rent seeking is wasteful, in some aggregative social evaluation.

In the majority rule game, the winners secure differential payoffs, the losers are exploited. This characteristic feature is present even if and when the participants make no rent-seeking investment at all. If the collective action involves any genuine publicness, on either the cost or benefit side (in the example of Figure 3.2, the participants share benefits in a genuinely public good), unconstrained majority rule may generate results that involve either too much or too little production of the public good in some aggregate utilitarian sense and as measured by cost–benefit equalization at the margin. (Note that, in Figure 3.2, the suggested majoritarian result in which outcomes rotate as among those three [marked by *M*s] that involve symmetrical sharing of gains as between members of majority coalitions, there will be only three units of public good per period provided, whereas the "efficient" result will involve six units per period.)

The conventional analysis here, based on traditional welfare economics models, neglects altogether the incentives that persons have to invest in efforts to secure membership in majority coalitions. Any such outlay of resources in rent-seeking activity reduces the net payoffs that individuals expect to secure from participation in the whole collective enterprise. Any estimate of the magnitude of rent-seeking costs, either for a single person or in the aggregate, is difficult to make, even in the simplest of models. Any expected gain from membership in a successful majority coalition may be less than or more than fully dissipated in efforts to ensure membership. And, of course, over a whole sequence of periods under majoritarian electoral rotation, the promised gains from collective action may be negatory.[1]

D. Differences in value product among persons

In the analysis of Section C, including the construction of the numerical example, all persons in the collective interaction are assumed to be identical in their evaluation of the public good because the schedule of product value is assumed identical for each person. (Each farmer's productivity is equally enhanced by drainage of the meadow.) The extension of the analysis to allow for differences in the evaluation of the commonly shared good is clearly indicated. How many of the generalized results depend critically on the presumed identity in the separate evaluations?

As the numerical example to be presented in Figure 3.4 suggests, the introduction of differences in orderings modifies the earlier result of neutrality of the decision rule even when constitutional restrictions allow for solutions only on the diagonal. Similarly, even within such constraints, the identity of the majority matters, along with the decision rule. And the presence of such constraints does not totally eliminate rent-seeking activity when evaluations differ as among participants. But there remains a critically important incentive difference between the diagonal and the off-diagonal models – a difference that guarantees much lower rent-seeking activity when the off-diagonal solutions are constitutionally out of bounds.

These conclusions may be illustrated in the payoff structure depicted in Figure 3.4, which incorporates differences among the three parties in their evaluation of the commonly shared good based on differences in productivity of this good. The assumption of identity in evaluation of inputs in production of the good is maintained.

In the construction of the example depicted in Figure 3.4, schedules for Individual *B* are presumed unchanged from those behind Figures 3.2 and 3.3. By comparison, the productivity of the public good is lower for Individual *A* and higher for Individual *C* than in the other constructions. All persons place the same value (negative) on inputs (as before). Productivity schedules are detailed in notes for Figure 3.4.

As in the earlier construction, we may divide the set of sixty-four possible outcomes into two subsets: (1) those that are majority dominated and (2) those that are

		W_3	W_2	W_1	W_0
		I	II	III	IV
		-9, 9, 36	-9, 22, 31	-10, 34, 25	-12, 45, 18
		-9, 7, 46	-10, 19, 40	-12, 30, 33	-15, 40, 25
	W_3	-10, 4, 55	-12, 15, 48	-15, 25, 40	-19, 34, 31
		-12, 0, 63	-15, 10, 55	-19, 19, 46	-24, 27, 36
		V	VI	VII	VIII
		6, 7, 31	5, 19, 25	3, 30, 18	0, 40, 10
		5, 4, 40	*3, 15, 33*	0, 25, 25	-4, 34, 16
	W_2	3, 0, 48	0, 10, 40	-4, 19, 31	-9, 27, 21
		0,- 5, 55	-4, 4, 46	-9, 12, 36	-15, 19, 25
A		IX	X	XI	XII
		20, 4, 25	18, 15, 18	15, 25, 10	11, 34, 1
		18, 0, 33	15, 10, 25	11, 19, 16	6, 27, 6
	W_1	15, -5, 40	11, 4, 31	*6, 12, 21*	0, 19, 10
		11, -11, 46	6, -3, 36	0, 4, 25	-7, 10, 13
		XIII	XIV	XV	XVI
		33, 0, 18	30, 10, 10	26, 19, 1	21, 27, -9
		30, -5, 25	26, 4, 16	21, 12, 6	15, 19, -5
	W_0	26, -11, 31	21, -3, 21	15, 4, 10	8, 10, -2
		21, -18, 36	15, -11, 25	8, -5, 13	*0, 0, 0*

Figure 3.4. Three person, public good illustration with differing evaluations.

The payoffs are computed as follows:
(1) Each unit of input is supplied at a cost of 15 units of opportunity value, constant over quantities and equal for all persons.
(2) Units of output, equally available for all persons, are measured one for one with units of input, with value products for *A, B,* and *C* as shown by the following linear schedules:

	A	B	C
Units of Output	Total Product Value	Total Product Value	Total Product Value
1	8	10	13
2	15	19	25
3	21	27	36
4	26	34	46
5	30	40	55
6	33	45	63
7	35	49	70
8	36	52	76
9	36	54	81

nondominated. The second set is depicted in Figure 3.5. Unconstrained majority rule will generate a cycle as among members of this nondominated set. In the construction of Figure 3.2, because of the assumption of identical preferences, persons are symmetrical in payoffs when equally situated. This feature makes outcomes that embody symmetry in payoffs between members of the majority coalition more likely to emerge. A comparable claim seems less convincing in the setting depicted in Figure 3.5, where symmetry in payoffs cannot be identified until cardinal measures are introduced.

As in the earlier construction, the four solutions on the three-dimensional diagonal (in bold typeface in Figure 3.4) do not appear in Figure 3.5. Each of these outcomes,

A \ B	W_3	W_2	W_1	W_0
W_3	I -10, 4, 55 -12, 0, 63	II -12, 15, 48 -15, 10, 55	III -12, 30, 33 -15, 25, 40 -19, 19, 46	IV -12, 45, 18 -15, 40, 25 -19, 34, 31 -24, 27, 36
W_2	V	VI	VII	VIII
W_1	IX 15, -5, 40 11, -11, 46	X	XI	XII 11, 34, 1
W_0	XIII 33, 0, 18 30, -5, 25 26, -11, 31 21, -18, 36	XIV 30, 10, 10	XV 26, 19, 1	XVI 21, 27, -9

Figure 3.5. Majority nondominated imputations from Figure 3.4.

which involve symmetrical collectively imposed behavioral adjustment as among all of the three persons, is majority dominated and would, therefore, never be advanced as an alternative for collective action by any potential majority coalition.

Note that, differently from the comparable on-diagonal set under identical evaluations (Figure 3.2), here the three participants no longer exhibit the same rank ordering of the members of the on-diagonal set. The separate orderings are as follows:

A	B	C
$w_1\ w_1\ w_1\ (6, 12, 21)$	$w_2\ w_2\ w_2\ (3, 15, 33)$	$w_3\ w_3\ w_3\ (-9, 9, 36)$
$w_2\ w_2\ w_2\ (3, 15, 33)$	$w_1\ w_1\ w_1\ (6, 12, 21)$	$w_2\ w_2\ w_2\ (3, 15, 33)$
$w_0\ w_0\ w_0\ (0, 0, 0)$	$w_3\ w_3\ w_3\ (-9, 9, 36)$	$w_1\ w_1\ w_1\ (6, 12, 21)$
$w_3\ w_3\ w_3\ (-9, 9, 36)$	$w_0\ w_0\ w_0\ (0, 0, 0)$	$w_0\ w_0\ w_0\ (0, 0, 0)$

If majority rule is constrained so as to restrict the alternatives to this set, individual B's preferences will be determinant, and the $w_2\ w_2\ w_2$ (3, 15, 33) imputation will be stable. The median voter theorem applies because all preferences are single peaked along the one dimension on the diagonal.

It seems clear that much of the public-choice analysis of single-peaked preferences and the median voter theorem has been based on the implicit assumption that the alternatives for majoritarian choice incorporate some attribute akin to the on-diagonal or symmetry property that is made explicit in the treatment here. In a generalized choice setting in which some endogeneity in the definition of the choice set must be acknowledged, symmetry imposes the equivalent of a unique dimension on a multidimensional space and thereby accomplishes the dual purposes of promoting majority stability and reducing rent-seeking investment. (More on these points later.)[2]

An alternative interpretation of the orthodox public-choice (and social-choice) theory of majority voting processes is less generous and suggests that this theory has simply presumed exogeneity in the definition of the majoritarian choice set. The distinction between exogeneity and endogeneity has been discussed previously in Chapter 2. We reintroduce it here to illustrate its applicability through the numerical examples. For any three (or more) of the configurations of actions, and related payoffs, shown in Figures 3.2 or 3.4, the presence or absence of a majority cycle resulting from a sequence of pairwise voting choices could be ascertained readily. And, if no cycle occurs, single peakedness would describe the preference orderings over the alternatives arrayed along the "dimension" arbitrarily constructed. However, much of such analysis becomes wasted effort once we recognize that the alternatives in the majoritarian choice set do not appear as if from "nature," but, instead, emerge from the prospective utility maximizing behavior of political entrepreneurs who themselves "invent" the alternatives. And, in this setting, as noted, the choice set generated endogenously must contain the majoritarian cycle in the absence of constraints.

E. Majority stability under on-diagonal constraints

We have noted previously that, in the numerical example depicted in Figure 3.4, under a constraint that requires symmetry or generality in the collectively chosen alternative (i.e., a constraint that restricts solutions to the northwest–southeast diagonal in the matrix), majority voting will produce a unique equilibrium at the alternative from the on-diagonal set preferred by the median voter. Is such a majority stability a property of the generality constraint, or does this particular result depend on the arbitrary design of the example?

We suggest that the on-diagonal constraint does indeed guarantee majority stability so long as individual orderings exhibit the standard convexity characteristics ordinarily used in economic theory. So long as the objectives for collective action can be interpreted as goods that enter individuals' utility functions and are available only at opportunity costs measured by other valued goods, and so long as voters' orderings exhibit constant or unidirectional changes in evaluation over quantities of inputs (outputs), single peakedness will describe the orderings over the alternatives arrayed along the diagonal.

Again, we illustrate the argument with the numerical example in Figure 3.4. The three persons, A, B, and C, exhibit negative and constant marginal evaluations (intrapersonally measured) for the supply of inputs in the production of the commonly shared public good. The marginal productivity of this good differs as among the three persons but declines with quantity for each person. Note that the majority equilibrium attained under these configurations might disappear and a cycle will emerge under pairwise majority voting, even among on-diagonal alternatives, if either marginal value product of the public good and/or the opportunity value of inputs for any person should exhibit directional reversal over the relevant range. Such phenomena would, however, contradict the basic behavioral postulates upon which economic theory rests.

Confronted with the orthodox analysis of majority voting, with its concentration on the likely emergence of cycles, Gordon Tullock (1981) asked, "Why so much stability?" in the politics that is empirically observed. The analysis developed here offers at least a partial answer. Although effective formal constraints restricting collective actions to those that embody generality in treatment among individuals and groups do not exist, the rhetoric of political discourse along with subsequent political action has been such that overt intergroup discrimination, based largely on majority–minority identification, may be less pervasive than the reductionist analytical models might suggest. The purely redistributive aspects of politics are, to an extent, sublimated to the generality features. It is widely accepted, however, that redistributional politics has become relatively more important over the course of the century, both as a causal and reactive element to the dramatic growth in the size of the public sector. The implied falsifiable hypothesis is that we should have predicted a temporal increase in the instability of majoritarian political processes.

F. The political efficiency of generality in a setting with preference differences

In the earlier model in which we assumed all persons exhibit identical preferences, analyzed in Section C and depicted in Figure 3.2, it was not perhaps surprising that the economically "efficient" solution (assuming interpersonally comparable payoffs) would lie along the diagonal and that departures from this solution that might be motivated by the discriminatory distributional opportunities offered by the operation of majority rule would involve aggregative losses. Even if we make the limiting assumption of zero transaction costs, which would allow for costless implementation of side payments, there is no Pareto-superior move that might be made from the equilibrium, regardless of the decision rule.

This feature of the analysis changes when the preferences of the participants differ because of differences in the productivity of the commonly shared public good among persons, or, possibly, because of differences in opportunity values of input supply. Here, the "optimally efficient" assignment might not be expected to embody symmetry as among the participants. In the stylized setting in which only economic efficiency is considered, any solution on the diagonal, which must incorporate symmetry, might be Pareto dominated by other solutions off the diagonal. Under the limiting assumption of zero transaction costs, when side payments may be costlessly organized and both input and output units are fully divisible, any on-diagonal imputation remains inefficient. Some reassignment of inputs (taxes) toward those who value public good outputs more highly might be worked out, with appropriately computed side payments, so as to benefit all parties.

Under these conditions, it would seem to be more difficult to make the argument for restricting the sets of possible outcomes to those that fall along the diagonal. Such an inference would, however, fail to take into account the difference in "political efficiency" that the two constitutional regimes embody. The results suggested previously depend on economic efficiency, defined in the standard way and in isolation from political efficiency. If the latter is taken into account properly, the argument for requiring symmetry or generality carries through without major change.

We use the term *political efficiency* to describe the efficacy of differing institutions in reducing or eliminating the incentives for participants to invest resources in rent seeking aimed to secure discriminatory advantage through majoritarian exploitation. An institution is defined to be maximally efficient, politically, when there are no incentives for any person to make such investment. As noted earlier, the on-diagonal restriction in the identical evaluation model meets this criterion, and we introduced this model as providing a benchmark for analysis. With differences in evaluations, the separate players may prefer differing solutions, even along the diagonal. And, although the median voter's preference will tend to be determining under normal settings, there will remain some incentive for nonmedian participants to invest in efforts to secure more favorable outcomes. In the example, Individual C will invest resources in efforts to shift the majoritarian solution toward a larger supply of the public good, whereas Individual A will make similar investment to exert pressures in the opposing direction.[3]

We suggest, however, that the incentives for shifts in the symmetrical solution along the diagonal remain minimal by comparison with those incentives that emerge under nonconstrained majority voting. The constitutional constraint that limits majoritarian solutions to those that lie along the diagonal increases, and by an order of magnitude that is significant, the political efficiency of the whole political regime also increases. Persons retain some incentives to invest in efforts to convince others to support their own preferred positions, but there remain no incentives for persons to seek membership in majority coalitions that are aimed specifically at discriminatory or differential advantage to the majority at the expense of members of the minority. The gains in political efficiency that the symmetry constraint ensures would seem to more than offset any possible loss in ideal or potential allocative efficiency, defined in the usual manner–an efficiency that could scarcely be realized under any recognizable political regime and certainly not in one that gives scope for the workings of majoritarian institutions.

4 Extending the argument

The simple interaction models introduced in earlier chapters share a common feature that must be examined further. In each setting, the participants are described by behavioral symmetry in the absence of or prior to collective action. The Nash equilibrium is reached when each person maximizes personal anticipated payoffs from independent or private action. This setting is, of course, familiar and is analyzed variously in the standard PD models of game theory, in the "tragedy of the commons," with Samuelsonian public goods phenomena. Our own example, that of David Hume's farmers who might join forces to drain the adjacent meadow, is broadly illustrative. In the terminology of Chapter 2, the models presume that the Nash or independent adjustment equilibrium is *on the diagonal* of the imaginary matrix. We must examine the extent to which this on-diagonal feature is important for the relevant normative conclusion concerning the efficiency of a generality constraint.

At this point it is useful to recall just what our analytical enterprise in this book is all about. Our normative concern is about *political* discrimination among separate persons and groups – discrimination that is reflected in unequal or differential treatment at the dictates of a governmental–collective authority, as guided by some decision rule or process. The generality norm, elaborated through the on-diagonal metaphor in earlier chapters, is aimed toward enforcing uniformity in political treatment for all persons in the polity. This norm does not, and should not, imply uniformity in behavior or actions by individuals in their private or noncollective spheres of activity. Outside the realm of collective action, individuals should be at liberty to act as they prefer, within the constraints that each one separately confronts.

A. The basis for collective action

The benchmark or base point from which to compare the possible efficacy of collective action is that position attained in the total absence of such action. Such a position, in a stylized sense, is familiarly known as the *Nash equilibrium* – the position that emerges from the simultaneous but separated choices made by all parties to the relevant interaction. A few, some, or many persons, finding themselves in a situation in which a valued but nonexcludable and commonly shared good, can, if necessary, be privately supplied, and may, in the absence of explicit collective organization, supply some inputs toward production. The central theorem of orthodox public goods analysis states that such private or independent adjustment (the market allocation) will generate an inefficiently low allocation of resources to the production of goods so characterized. But this theorem should not and does not carry the inference that, in the absence of collective action, no resources are devoted to the production–supply of such goods or that all beneficiaries behave uniformly toward its provision.

Consider, again, our much-used example: Hume's farmers who live alongside the meadow. If the benefits from drainage are sufficiently high, we might expect that some effort toward producing the public good will be forthcoming, even prior to any collectivization. And, if the productivity or personal evaluation of the good differs as among the members of the sharing group, we should also expect to observe differing quantities of privately directed effort.

The pre-collectivized position, the Nash equilibrium, is the appropriate benchmark with which any collectivized result must be compared. And it is analytically legitimate to characterize this position as being *symmetrical* with reference to *inputs* supplied under collective direction. No participant supplies an input under the directed coercion of a collective authority for the simple reason that no such authority is in being. The logical model for collective action, depicted in a matrix or any other metaphor, includes prospective results that may be generated by the provision of positive quantities of inputs by participants, under the direction of the collectivity, quite apart from any private or voluntary effort, either in the absence or presence of explicit collective action. And, of course, there will exist predicted possible feedback effects between collective action, if any, and private supply choices.

B. The meaning of symmetry

It is relatively easy to discuss symmetry or generality in the context of highly stylized abstract models, such as those analyzed in Chapter 3. It becomes much more difficult to make the argument itself more general. Even if we succeed in defining the benchmark, as in the previous section, it remains necessary to clarify the meaning of generality or symmetry in political treatment. This elementary step must be taken before we can classify positions as on or off some diagonal, in terms of our inclusive matrix metaphor.

The definitional issue is operationally important for our normative analytical enterprise because we want the generality principle to be sufficiently inclusive to apply meaningfully as an effective constitutional constraint on majoritarian politics. As several of the particular applications discussed in later chapters demonstrate, it may be easier to identify violations of the generality norm than it is to lay out precise conditions for adherence. Nonetheless, an effort must be made, lest the whole exercise be accused of lacking any analytical bridge to political reality.

What, precisely, does it mean to say that separate persons are treated symmetrically in politics? We must, of course, acknowledge personal differences among individuals in many attributes, characteristics, or qualities, whether their origins be genetic, environmental, stochastic, or voluntaristic. As they are conceived to enter into or remain within political community, however, there is a sense in which persons are nominal equals. Such equality is presumed, both in some normative and some positive sense, by the universality and equality of the voting franchise in democracy.

Why do persons enter into or remain within a political community? Democracy, as such, loses its *raison d'être* if politics, so organized, becomes, and is seen to become, nothing more than a means through which one coalition of persons (groups) succeeds in extracting value from another coalition. Democratic politics takes on normative significance only if some "common good" is postulated. In this sense at least, the traditional political theorists have been correct. Their efforts have often been misleading, however, because of their continuing search for external sources for defining such common good. The contractarian alternative locates the definitional source in the evaluations of individual participants. Commonality arises from the technology of production and usage of the bundle of commonly valued goods and services that are collectivized. Persons enter a political community because they expect to enhance their own well-being by sharing in the collective enterprise that is itself described by the terms of exchange, on both sides of the account, between individuals and the collectivity.

Within this basic contractarian understanding of democratic politics, it is relatively easy to define generality or symmetry on that side of the account that is expected to be utility enhancing to the individual participant. A collectively financed and/or supplied good or service, or bundle, must be generally available to all members of the political unit, whether the nonexcludability feature is inherent in the technology of delivery itself or it is explicitly constructed. The generality norm is clearly violated when a collectively financed program is aimed explicitly to offer benefits to some members of the polity to the exclusion of others. Note, however, that this requirement does not imply that a collectively financed good or service yield measurably equal flows of physical output to separate persons, or that all persons place comparable values on such flows (Buchanan, 1968). A generally available good or service may be valued differentially by separate persons and for either or both of these reasons. Generality is violated, however, when, as, and if access to the good or service is denied, thereby forestalling any possible evaluation.

Problems in defining generality become much more difficult when attention is shifted to the side of the individual's account with the collectivity that involves expected utility reduction. There is no "publicness," "nonexcludability," or "commonality" in the allocation of shares in the costs of political or collective action. Individually measured shares must be assigned politically, and it is centrally the conflictual elements in all such assignments that create the opportunities for majoritarian exploitation against which the generality principle is alleged to operate. But what allocations or sets of allocations here qualify as meeting the generality norm? What allocations must be rejected?

Recall the purpose of our whole effort here as summarized in the first sentence of the second paragraph of this section. If we define generality too narrowly, we are likely to rule out the potential usefulness of the norm in any practical constitutional application. But also recall the discussion in the previous section, in which the attribute of symmetry was assigned to the Nash equilibrium or precollective position, despite the existence of predicted differences in voluntary supply behavior. Persons are, in fact, unequals as they enter into the collective enterprise, and they remain so in their private behavioral reactions. What then may be implied about their relative treatment within the operation of the political–collective enterprise itself?

We need to unpack the problem more carefully. Somewhere along an imaginary spectrum between objectively measurable equality and overtly discriminatory and politically imposed inequality a dividing line may be drawn, on one side of which the generality criterion may be deemed to be satisfied and on the other side of which such a criterion may be deemed to be violated. In a conjecturally empirical setting, the criterion may be defined self-referentially. If persons, drawn from both majority and minority coalitions in positions of dominance through a sequence of periods, accept the allocations of political burdens to be broadly "fair" or "just," the generality norm may be judged to be met. And, relationally, such acceptance would be observed in practice by the absence of dramatic shifts in cost allocations as political majorities rotate over sequential electoral cycles.

Neither of these related definitions is, however, helpful in designing a constitutional constraint independently and in advance – a constraint that will limit majoritarian exploitation and, at the same time, will facilitate majoritarian efficiency in generating collective action toward advancing the well-being of all participants.

We seek a measure – a yardstick – that may be used to compare persons, one with another, as participants in political association, and, particularly, as subjects to coercion by collective authority. How does the political treatment accorded to one person compare with that accorded to another, and especially as we recognize that persons differ in their capacities as well as their preferences? Considered abstractly, the generality principle has great normative appeal, but how do we translate the principle into political reality?

We may, first of all, note that the problem is not at all difficult in many settings for collective action, where there is a natural meaning of generality. For example, consider military conscription. Clearly, the generality norm here requires that all persons, in a well-defined age bracket, be accorded like treatment. (It was the apparent violation of generality in the Vietnam era draft that offered the source of much of the antiwar agitation.) Other examples such as curfews, zoning, and criminal sentencing may also fall within this classification in which generality in treatment is not hard to define so as to command near-universal assent.

Major definitional issues arise, however, once we try to apply the generality norm to distribution of fiscal burden. In the simple example introduced in Chapter 3, we used labor time as the appropriate measure for comparison. The inputs of the participants were classified as weeks of work toward producing the commonly shared good, on the presumption that the separate farmers were equally productive. But what if one person, say A, should be twice as productive as B or C? What does equal treatment mean in this setting? What defines a position to be on the diagonal of the matrix?

Let us stay with the example here and suppose that we postulate that the generality principle is met when separate participants make equal contributions measured by units of valued output rather than equal contributions measured by units of input. In this case, Person A, who is two times as productive as Person B or Person C, would be judged to have met the equal obligation by working only one-half the time spent by peers. In this setting, Person A secures the full benefits of the commonly shared good at a lower personal outlay than the others. Such an arrangement seems to run counter to common-sense notions of equality or symmetry.

Adam Smith (1937/1776) faced the same problem – that of finding a meaningful measure of value that could be used to apply across persons with differing qualities – although his purpose in this quest was quite different from the one that motivates our analysis here. Smith's solution was that "equal quantities of labour, at all times and places, may be said to be of equal value to the labourer" (p. 33). We suggest that Smith's measure is also useful for our purposes. In the political enterprise, broadly considered, persons may be deemed to be treated in accord with the generality norm when their coerced exactions in payment for sharing do not depart significantly from equality in the labor time required to meet these exactions. For example, a tax-sharing scheme satisfies the generality norm when the person who earns $120,000 annually is subjected to a tax of $10,000, whereas the person who earns $12,000 annually is taxed for $1,000. This collectively imposed scheme requires that each person donate the equivalent of one-month's income for financing the jointly shared public good.

But how can the generality principle be extended to apply to persons who share in the availability of the collectively supplied good or service, as members of the political community, but who participate in the economic nexus, in whole or in part, as rentiers, who do not earn labor incomes? It seems plausibly acceptable to treat rentier income as if it is earned from labor applied uniformly over the relevant time periods. With this readjustment of measure, the labor–time yardstick allows for a ready conversion into relative charges against a broad tax base such as income. (For further discussion, see Chapter 8.)

With this relatively inclusive, but still objectifiable, definition of symmetry in political treatment, we have, in effect, located the diagonal of the *n*-dimensional matrix in such a way as to make the enterprise of collective action meaningful for purposes of constitutional constraints on majoritarian impulses. A rough matching of politically imposed burdens with labor–time equivalents would not be viewed to be grossly exploitative by members of any group, and collectivization of many activities may be potentially value enhancing under this restriction, thereby commanding support that would not be forthcoming under nonconstrained majoritarian processes.

C. Constitutionalization as generalization

Many of the desired results that stem from satisfaction of the generality principle in politics may be achieved even if our previous-section efforts to define symmetry–equality in treatment of persons are rejected. A procedural, rather than a substantive, approach may be suggested, and one that does not require some prior definition of what the generality norm requires. *Constitutionalization*, in itself, may be sufficient to ensure that many of the objectives of generality are obtained.

It is useful to examine more specifically what constitutionalization will accomplish. Consider Figure 4.1, in which the collectively imposed input requirements for producing–supplying a commonly shared good are measured separately along each personalized dimension, with, once again, the two-person model being used to illustrate the large-number interaction setting. The base point or origin at E is the Nash equilibrium, where the two persons, A and B, are symmetrical in their collectivized behavior patterns; neither supplies input at the direction of collective authority. (Each may, or may not, supply inputs independently in the Nash equilibrium and may, of course, voluntarily supplement collective supply after politicization of the activity.)

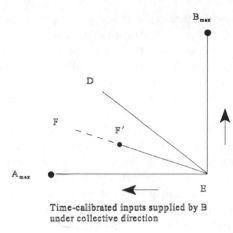

Figure 4.1. Efficiency beyond generality.

Assume, now, that there exists no position along the standard diagonal, ED, that is value-enhancing over that at E, for both persons. (No Pareto-superior move from E to a position on ED is possible.) If restricted to the subset of positions along this diagonal, there would never be a constitutional agreement for collectivization of the activity, regardless of the decision rule. In the example, we may suppose that A does not find the commonly shared (and valued) good sufficiently productive to induce any contribution to its supply if symmetry in time-calibrated inputs is a required condition.

Suppose, however, that there do exist positions that generate mutual gains from those present at E, provided that the inputs are supplied disproportionately. In such case, constitutional agreement on collectivization might be reached, provided that some assurance could be given that politics would, in fact, allow effective choices to be limited to the subset of value-enhancing positions. Suppose, however, it is known, in advance, that any position in such a subset is majority-dominated by other positions, none of which involves value enhancement for all members of the polity. (See the discussion of majority dominance in Chapter 3.)

For illustration, in Figure 4.1, suppose that positions along the line segment EF' are value enhancing for both A and B. In this case, a constitutional stipulation that the two persons, A and B, are to contribute inputs in the fixed ratio indicated by the slope of the vector EF will ensure that collective authority will not be exploitative in treatment of either of the parties. In this setting, rotation of decision authority between A and B will involve some shifting among positions that lie within the EF' subset.

As we expand the number of participants in the collective-sharing group (the number of dimensions in the model), constitutionalization of the input-sharing arrangements, along with a majority voting rule to determine budgetary size, will restrict alternatives to those that lie along the single n-dimensional vector. And from these alternatives, that which reflects median voter preferences will emerge and will be majority stable.

Note, specifically, what constitutionalization, as such, accomplishes in this setting. In the two-person model depicted in Figure 4.1, unconstrained rotation of collective decision authority between the two parties (analogous to majoritarian electoral cycles) would involve continuous switching among positions such as those shown at A_{max} and B_{max}, which represent, in each case, maximal in-period exploitation of one person by another, within the limits of the particular collective action examined. Constitutionally constrained decision authority would place limits on such exploitation, in any period, and would act so as to ensure that the activity in question remains value-enhancing for all parties.

It is also clear, for the same reasons that were noted earlier, that constitutionalization of cost-sharing arrangements, even if the relative shares cannot be defined to be symmetrical in the standard sense, tends to minimize wasteful investment of resources in majoritarian rent seeking. In the context of our matrix constructions, constitutionalization may be interpreted as a displacement and relocation of the politically relevant diagonal, so as to reflect the n-dimensional generality that matches the political as well as the psychological reality of the sharing community.

Constitutionalization of the burden–share arrangements effectively separates the two sides of the collective decision and, in so doing, reduces dramatically the scope for distributionally motivated in-period politics. Recognition of this result may have led Hayek to suggest a two-chamber legislative structure with burden–share allocation authority lodged in an "upper" chamber and ordinary budgetary authority assigned to a "lower" body (Hayek, 1960). Brennan and Buchanan (1981a; Brennan, 1987) have also stressed the political efficacy of treating the tax system as "social overhead capital." Their arguments tend to support constitutionalization, as such, and quite apart from any direct relationship to the generality norm.

D. Generality and the justification for collective action

We have discussed the generality principle, and its procedural derivative, constitutionalization, on the implicit presumption that the origins and continuing justification for political community are found in some contractarian enterprise that involves cooperative sharing aimed to achieve commonly valued results. In this setting, the generality norm has as its central purpose the imposition of constraints or limits on the operation of majority rule politics. In effect, constitutionalization of a collective activity amounts to a quasi-permanent implementation of the results of the more inclusive decision rule as a means of forestalling specifically the predicted departures from such results under majority rule. There may exist specific activities that embody departures from generality in treatment among persons and groups that might command substantial or even complete agreement as evaluated behind some veil of ignorance/uncertainty, both on collective organization and operation. At the same time, collectivization of such activities might not be justified, even on idealized veil-of-ignorance criteria, on the presumption that in-period decisions are to be made by majoritarian processes. In these circumstances, constitutionalization offers a possible means of securing the promised efficiencies of nongeneral collective actions without the predicted costs that stem from majoritarian exploitation.

Care must be taken, however, not to allow for or acknowledge a defense of majoritarian exploitation under a guise that the generality norm is satisfied. If activities are collectivized that cannot be value-enhancing to all persons under any allocation of burden (if there are no Pareto-superior movements from the Nash equilibrium), the satisfaction of the generality criterion carries little normative content and may, in practice, be value-reducing for some participants.

Return to the illustration in Figure 4.1. If there are no vectors from E that include positions in which the expected utility payoffs are higher than those at E, and for all members of the community, then there is no justification for collectivization of the activity in question. And, in this case, there is no substantive normative content in the argument that solutions should lie along the diagonal or even that the burden-sharing arrangements should be constitutionalized. In either case, rent-seeking waste would be minimal, but any and all positions within the on-diagonal, or constitutionalized, subset involve net loss for some participants in the political community.

The precautionary point at issue here becomes especially relevant when there is some subversion or usurpation of genuine constitutional authority by members of a potential majority coalition who share a conviction that some private activities are behaviorally bad and should be prohibited politically or penalized. In the historical experience of the United States, the Prohibitionists in 1919 were quite willing to extend the law generally to all citizens; that is, to impose solutions that lie along the diagonal in our analytical construction. The Prohibitionists did not seek overtly to use political authority to capture distributional advantage. But the satisfaction of the generality principle, as such, did not serve to justify, even if indirectly, the collectivization–politicization of an activity that should have been left outside the public sector.

This example suggests that the generality precept, as such, must always be introduced with some care. Properly applied, its purpose is to ensure that "good politics" is kept within bounds. Generality, as a feature of "bad politics" may or may not be desirable, and should not, ever, be invoked as a justification for illegitimate political coercion.

5   Generality and the political agenda

Preceding chapters have been aimed to provide a foundational understanding of and an elementary appreciation for the principle of generality in the politics of democracy. The argument has been developed largely through a series of highly abstract and grossly simplified examples; many critics would perhaps reject the reductionism involved. The purpose of this chapter is different. We shall discuss the relationship of generality to the agenda of political democracy. What conception of politics, as an inclusive enterprise, is required for the generality norm to become a relevant attribute? How does this conception differ from alternative, and possibly more familiar, understandings? Why has the *unnatural* feature of generality been neglected? What have been the implicit assumptions that have allowed analysts to presume generality where it does not, and indeed cannot, exist?

Responses to these and other like questions suggest a direct linkage between the generality norm and constitutional structure. Although it may seem to be a digression, critical attention must be paid to the implicit understandings in theoretical welfare economics and particularly in the implications for constitutional politics. How can "choices among social states," a central focus of orthodox analysis, be related to the generality precepts stressed in this book?

The discussion may prompt an offsetting inquiry. Given the unnatural relationship between generality and majoritarian politics, along with the failure of analysts, engaged in both positive and normative exercises, to place such an attribute in any central role, why do we observe any adherence to the principle of generality at all in the politics that we observe?

Here we once again return to the intersection between law and politics. Political action is effectuated through legal action, through changes in laws. Established law imposes checks on the raw exercise of political departures from the generality precepts. In one sense, law, as embodied in both formal structures and public understanding, forces political decision makers, who would discriminate among persons and groups in the polity, to justify their actions in a rhetoric of public interest to be pursued without overt violations of vaguely defined rights claimed by persons. These constraints, in turn, act to ensure that political discrimination occurs along the intersections of large groups and classes of persons that may be described locationally, financially, organizationally, professionally, industrially, or behaviorally rather than among separate persons, as such, and as they might be politically classified. The "rule of law," as traditionally interpreted, stays the hand of those politicians representing majority coalitions from differentiating in detail, among persons and groups, in terms of what would be considered to be arbitrary criteria of classification, such as race, gender, or religion. The differentiation that is considered to be out of bounds may, of course, vary over time and place. But the point is that the principle of legal treatment, as it has operated, restricts the discriminatory potential inherent in majoritarian politics.

Interestingly enough, we witness, in the last decade of the century, arguments that support departures from generality based on alleged benefits of diversity – arguments that remain totally uninformed by the elementary logic of majoritarian politics.

A. Politics as paradigm

Public-choice theory is touted by its proponents and practitioners as embodying a nonromantic vision of politics in its positive variants. But explanation is not enough, and some justificatory argument is required to offer legitimacy for political coercion. The "politics as complex exchange" paradigm is intellectually–evaluatively attractive in this respect because it does indeed provide such putative legitimacy for the explicitly political restrictions on the liberties of individuals, who are presumed to remain parties to the generalized constitutional contract that establishes the rules within which political choices are made.

Constitutional political economy, inclusively interpreted, seeks to explain and understand basic constitutional choices in some ultimate metaphor of exchange, some model of generalized agreement on rules, possibly derived from an individual calculus of interest carried out behind some appropriately defined veil of ignorance and/or uncertainty. At the same time, the parties to constitutional agreement are presumed to model in-period or within-rules politics as conflict rather than exchange. If a majority decision rule is treated as the selected means of making in-period choices, analysis then proceeds on the accepted presumption that majority coalitions maximize utilities for members through exploiting minorities to the extent that is constitutionally feasible. In the basic analysis of the choice among decision rules, which was the focus of inquiry in *The Calculus of Consent* (Buchanan and Tullock, 1962), there is no logical dominance of majority rule for in-period political decisions. And the potential avenues for constitutional reform may include more inclusive rules, along lines of argument originating with Wicksell (1896).

As we have noted on several occasions, however, the starting point for the whole analysis in this book is not defined by placing the citizen in some stylized constitutional convention in which there is a choice among alternative decision rules, only one of which is the rule of majority. Instead, here we bow to the equivalence of democracy and majority rule in attitudes exhibited both by the citizenry and academic intellectuals. We acknowledge, albeit reluctantly, that modern democratic politics will be and must remain majoritarian in one or another of its many institutional variations. If we seek to reform the structure, we must do so within the limits dictated by the operation of majority rule.

It is from this context that our emphasis on the generality principle or norm emerges. Again, we place the citizen, whom we treat as our ultimate addressee, at a point of constitutional choice. But this time, the citizen confronts a choice, not among differing decision rules but among alternative institutional constraints that may be placed on the exercise of majoritarian politics, modeled in terms of the utility maximizing behavior of participants. The constitutional requirement that all political action be general in applicability, over all members of the political community, is the exclusive focus of our analysis.

B. Generality as unnatural

The highly abstract analytical exercises in Chapters 3 and 4 emphasize that generality in treatment among persons is not at all a *natural* feature of majoritarian politics. As we have mentioned earlier, majority rule means that members of the minority are ruled; that is, treated in a differential or discriminatory fashion by comparison with members of the majority. Generality or nondiscrimination in treatment, as among all members of the polity, must be classified to be an unnatural feature in any model in which individual behavior is postulated to be rational and utility maximizing. In the absence of constraints, it becomes behaviorally *nonfeasible* for persons to forego opportunities to increase their own utility payoffs.

The relationship between behavioral feasibility as a meaningful limitation on the set of predicted political outcomes and the place of the generality norm under majority rule warrants further discussion, and especially as interpreted in Paretian welfare economics. As the simple models in Chapter 4 indicated, there may exist political outcomes that satisfy both the generality norm and the Pareto criterion that may also be reached by Pareto-superior reforms from some precollectivization status quo. Such outcomes may be dominated, however, for all members of a majority coalition, by others that do not exhibit generality, and that, although satisfying the Pareto criterion once reached, are attained only by a change that violates Pareto superiority.

Paretian welfare economists are reluctant to relegate outcomes that are majority dominated to the set classified to be nonfeasible. The temptation remains strong to model majoritarian politics as if some feature analogous to the unanimity rule remains operative. The logical structure of majority rule, which requires nongenerality in its effects, is often not sufficiently persuasive to sweep away all elements of idealism.

C. The myth of publicness

Part of the problem here, at least in explaining the apparent unwillingness of welfare economists to abandon many prospects as behaviorally nonfeasible, lies in the separate, but related, development of the theory of public goods, initially formalized as a theory of public expenditure by Paul A. Samuelson in his seminal 1954 paper. Samuelson's aim was to define rigorously the necessary conditions that must be satisfied for economic efficiency in the allocation of resources to the supply of goods that are collectively consumed by all members of a political community. In the stylized model, collective or joint consumption is presumably dictated by the technological characteristics of the goods, specifically those of nonrivalry and nonexcludability. One way of defining a good or service that fully meets the definitional standard here is to point to the total absence of a distributional component in its usage (Buchanan, 1968). The technology itself ensures that no sharing or partitioning problem could arise.

The absence of a distributional component applies, however, only along the dimension that measures the quantity of the good or service that exhibits publicness in the sense defined. The formal Samuelson model tends to obscure the distributional component that may arise on the reciprocal side of any allocative account. A good or service that fully meets the definitional requirements for publicness, and that is positively valued by potential users, does not emerge, exogenously as it were, from nature itself. Any such good or service must be supplied, and resource inputs are required for its production. The financing of production is partitionable among members of the collectivity. There exist many sharing arrangements that will cover the financing of any quantity of the commonly shared good or service. And differences among these arrangements (tax share allocations) are exclusively distributional.

The distribution of tax or cost shares for the production–supply of a collectively shared good or service need not be of central importance if the purpose of the analytical exercise is limited to the definition of the formal conditions for efficiency in resource use. As is well-known, however, this exercise suggests that decentralized, privatized, or market organization may fail to meet the efficiency standards. And the distributional features move to center stage when it is recognized that the whole logic of collective consumption–usage suggests the institutionalization of production–supply through political agency.

The distributional component that must be present in the financing dimension, even when collective action is limited to provision of goods and services that meet criteria for publicness, suggests that the natural thrust of majoritarian politics toward discriminatory treatment remains. The concentration of analysis, and analysts, on the nondistributional or publicness dimensions of adjustment may, however, have been important in distracting attention away from the potential for distributional conflict.

With reference to the analysis in earlier chapters, undue concentration on publicness features may have generated an implicit presumption that political alternatives necessarily lie along the diagonal; that is, that generality or nondiscrimination remains descriptive of political action, and for technological reasons. However, as the simple illustration of Hume's meadow demonstrates, off-diagonal results will emerge under majority rule, despite the genuine publicness of the good that is collectively provided.

The implicit presumption that the alternatives on the political agenda embody generality or nondiscrimination (i.e., that these alternatives lie along the diagonal) can only emerge from a model in which genuine publicness describes the dimensions along which the alternatives of potential collective action that might be selected by a majority are arranged. If there is no production required, as such, that is, if the good to be shared in common exists independently of individual behavior in bringing such a good into being but is subject to quantity adjustment, there are no actions that may differentially impact on the interacting parties. Different users may, of course, have differing preferences as to preferred quantities. Consider an example. Two persons share sleeping quarters; the thermostat must be set at a single number. There may be disagreement over the setting; the parties are in conflict over some range; the solution will depend on the decision rule. But, once settled, both parties must live with the same temperature.

If we expand the example to allow three or more persons to enter the publicness interaction, and if the preferences of each person are unidirectional around her bliss point, majority voting will ensure that the solution most desired by the person with the median preference emerges. And this position will be stable, despite the fact that it will not be preferred by many of the participants. If the preferences of one or more persons are not unidirectional around bliss points (in the example, if one or more persons prefer both a low and high thermostat setting to a setting in the middle), there will be no stable solution under majority voting.

The summary analysis here will be familiar to those exposed to elementary public-choice theory. Our purpose is not that of elaborating principles of majority voting. Instead, our purpose is the indirect one of indicating that the basic models of majority voting, upon which such a large share of public- and social-choice analysis is constructed, depend critically on the implicit assumption of publicness along the dimension of adjustment – an assumption that simply cannot be supported logically or institutionally. And even the presumption of publicness will not rescue the orthodoxy when and if we extend the model to multidimensions in which each dimension exhibits publicness separately.

The presumptive publicness of the alternatives in the political choice set amounts to a myth emergent from public- and social-choice methodology. It is relatively easy to understand how the myth gained its hold in the mind-set of so many sophisticated analysts. The alternatives for political–collective choice have been presumed to exist quite independently from the rule through which choices are made. And, at the most abstracted level of inquiry, these alternatives are inclusively defined as social states. As such, the alternatives become complete descriptions of the whole social order. In this conceptualization, it should have seemed obvious that a social state, as such, can only be modeled formally as a multidimensional vector. And, although it has been acknowledged that values for this vector that best meet the preferences of a majority coalition will be chosen as the political outcome, there has been little or no recognition given to the fact that the choice set is itself constructed by the decisive coalition, thereby ensuring against any fixed relationship among components of the n-dimensional vector that defines the alternatives. Partial exceptions to this generalized critique are represented only in the theories of platform selection in spatial voting analysis and in the theories of agenda selection and control.

D. The creativity of political choice

How do the alternatives among which collective choices are made come into being? Perhaps we may begin to answer this question by reference to a market analogy. How do the alternatives among which market choices are made come into being? Conventional wisdom comes up short in its failure to provide a ready answer. Implicitly and unthinkingly, economists often proceed as if the ultimate objects for choice – the end items that are valued for final usage – exist independently in nature, so to speak. Even in the 1990s, analytical exercises, our own included, refer to apples, oranges, deer, and beaver, as if these units are naturally defined. Simple observation suggests something quite different. The objects for market choice are themselves created by entrepreneurs who seek to satisfy preferences that can scarcely be said to exist independently of such creative effort. The ongoing and emerging process of interaction between individuals' preferences and the goods and services that meet such preferences is energized by the creative activity of entrepreneurs.

This analogy with market choice suggests that attention be paid to political entrepreneurship in the definition of the end items among which political or collective choices are made. Again, and more or less implicitly, conventional analysis has embodied the assumption that the choice set exists independently and is not, itself, constructed or created. Observation, as well as logical inquiry, suggests something different. Political entrepreneurship is as real, and as relevant, as market entrepreneurship, and creative effort is involved in setting up end objects that are anticipated to yield value to those who must, finally, exercise choice. We may, indeed, suggest that political entrepreneurship is relatively more important than its market counterpart because of the necessary mutual exclusiveness of political alternatives.

We must attend to the procedures or rules for making political choices, and we must recognize the interdependence between such rules and the activity of political entrepreneurs. Consider, first, a rule of unanimity. In this setting, the political entrepreneur, and his economist advisers, will necessarily search for, and construct, prospective alternatives to the political status quo that incorporate promised utility gains to all members of the constituency. By contrast, consider majority rule. The political entrepreneur will, again, search for, and construct, prospective alternatives that promise utility gains, but this time only for members of the majority coalition that may be formed. There is a dramatic difference between this model of majoritarian politics and that which describes the setting for conventional analysis in public choice. Exogenous alternatives, x and y, do not exist out there to be ordered in terms of preferences and one of the two finally chosen by majority voting in a pairwise comparison. Surely a more relevant model involves a political entrepreneur who constructs a package, x', that is hypothesized to elicit the preferences of some majority over the status quo, y', with the hypothesis put to the test in a vote.

If this latter model does isolate relevant features of political process, the presumption must be that all feasible alternatives are discriminatory in the sense that members of the decisive coalition secure differentially favored treatment. Generality in treatment, as between members of a majority and remaining members of the polity, violates the elementary behavioral postulates. Political entrepreneurs who might propose options that exhibit generality will not succeed in organizing majorities because any majority favoring a general proposal will switch to a nongeneral one offering even larger benefits once the latter proposal has been made.

E. Constitutional entrepreneurship

We have emphasized that the choice alternatives are themselves constructed by political entrepreneurs and that these alternatives depend on the rules through which political–collective decisions are made. Reference was also made earlier to the setting in which the choice alternatives might exhibit publicness, along a single relevant dimension, as technologically determined, in which case entrepreneurs, and their constituents, are necessarily prevented from exploiting the potential advantages from discrimination that majority rule seems to offer. We have acknowledged that it is difficult to think of examples that fit such a descriptive category of political action. The analysis remains, nonetheless, useful when we recognize that "constitutional publicness" can be introduced as a direct substitute for "technological publicness."

Consider, any stylized Samuelsonian public good that exhibits technological publicness on the benefits side of the allocative account but that can only be produced through some supply of privately partitionable inputs. Majority rule collectivization of the interaction will ensure discrimination between majority and minority members. Constitutional constraints may, however, be imposed, and these may substitute for the missing technological element on the financing or input dimension. If inputs can only be supplied, by constitutional mandate, so as to exhibit generality in treatment, permissible solutions must lie along the diagonal.

There is no explicit distributional discrimination, as such, despite the unchanged central role of majority voting in choosing among the constitutionally permitted set of options. In this setting, political entrepreneurs are, of course, restricted in the alternatives that qualify for inclusion in the majoritarian choice set. As the stylized illustrations in Chapter 3 demonstrated, however, majority rule differs categorically from unanimity rule, even in the restricted domain. Political entrepreneurs will seek to construct alternatives that are predicted to be preferred by members of a prospective majority, and differing majorities may prefer differing alternatives, despite the requirement that all permissible ones exhibit generality. Outcomes will emerge that meet the generality norm, and members of outvoted minorities will find their preferences thwarted. Note, however, that the failure of imposed solutions to meet minorities' first preference remains categorically different from overt discrimination. Care must be taken to distinguish, both analytically and in practice, between failure of majoritarian politics to satisfy minority preferences and explicit discrimination, as such, directed against minority interests. Again the point may be illustrated by reference to students who share living quarters. Having to sleep in a sixty-degree room because others prefer this temperature is quite different from having to sleep in an unheated attic while others enjoy heated spaces.

We have not yet addressed the question as to how a generality constraint might be constitutionally put in place. To demonstrate that such a constraint, if in place, would indeed work effectively as "artificial publicness" and, in so doing, act to eliminate the naturally discriminatory elements from majoritarian politics, does nothing toward explaining how such a constitutional constraint might come into being. Whose utility will be increased by the imposition and subsequent enforcement of an effective constitutional requirement for generality as an attribute of permissible political alternatives? Initially, it would seem that the activity of entrepreneurship here is categorically different from that for in-period or within-rule majority politics, discussed previously. Prospective gains cannot be reckoned to emerge, either from discriminatory exploitation or from more adequate meeting of majority preferences. Prospective gains from a generality constraint, to be imposed constitutionally, must themselves be general. Constitutional entrepreneurs would seem, therefore, unable to act strictly on behalf of a majority coalition.

Consider the calculus of an entrepreneur, who represents the interests of a prospective majority coalition, in evaluating constitutional alternatives. Suppose that this entrepreneur knows that, under existing rules, the majority can exploit the minority by imposing differentiation in treatment. Suppose that a change is under consideration that would impose the generality norm and that such a change would require minority assent. If the majority in being expects to remain permanently in a position of authority, no change in the constitutional rules can possibly seem beneficial. Suppose,

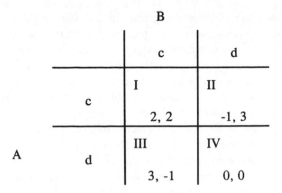

Figure 5.1. Efficiency of generality.

however, that the entrepreneur, who acts for the majority, recognizes that electoral rotation, under existing electoral rules that are constitutionally embedded, must almost surely guarantee elevation of current minorities to majority status in subsequent periods, with consequent discrimination against members of the now-dominant majority. That is to say, the current-period gains from discrimination against members of minorities will be recognized to be reversed in subsequent electoral sequences. In this setting, it may become rational for the members of the ruling majority coalition to support the constitutional change that will incorporate the generality principle, even in the understanding that adoption of such a rule will mean foregoing current period gains from discriminatory exploitation.

As illustration, look at the simple two-party interaction depicted in Figure 5.1, in which payoffs are treated as intrapersonally comparable measures of utility. Suppose that the interaction is collectivized and that Person A is in a position of authority in Period 1. The outcome in Cell III is dominant in the absence of any rule that requires generality. Suppose, however, that A expects that the decision authority will rotate evenly between A and B, on an expected value basis, over a continuing sequence of electoral periods, with solutions alternating evenly between Cells III and II. Hence, A expects to experience a payoff sequence: $3, -1, 3, -1, 3, -1, \ldots$ It is clear that under plausible values for discount rates, A may prefer that the generality constraint be implemented, because under this constraint the sequence $2, 2, 2, 2, \ldots$ is ensured. The arithmetical values in the illustration are, of course, rigged so as to emphasize the point to be made. But so long as there are, in net, efficiency losses involved in departures from generality, the rational bases for agreement on the constraint become clear. The current-period gains from exploitation are traded off in exchange for the insurance that the future period losses from reverse exploitation will be avoided.

Note what is and what is not suggested in the simple illustrative example. The unconstrained operation of the majoritarian political process may be, but need not be, damaging to all persons in order for the Pareto superiority of a generality constraint to hold. Consider, again, the values of the payoffs in Figure 5.1. If the decision-making authority is evenly rotated, the political game yields a value of one to each player, whereas the no-action status quo yields nothing. But the adoption of the generality constraint increases the value to two. Note, also, that the prospective gains need not be symmetrical in order for the generality constraint to be Pareto superior.

The whole analysis is designed to suggest that the observed operation of majoritarian politics, to the extent that it is described to be discriminatory as among differing members of the political community, is unlikely to be utility enhancing, relative to results generated under a generality constraint, to members of *any* prospective coalition so long as roughly equal prospects for electoral success in subsequent periods exist. That is to say, a generality constraint seems genuinely to be in the public interest. Note particularly that there need be no psychological transformation on the part of the ruling coalition members – no transformation that involves some deliberate shift to a position behind some veil of ignorance or uncertainty. What is required is that constitutional alternatives be reckoned in present-value accounting; myopic majorities would never agree to generality constraints (Levy, 1995).

Nonmyopic majorities may, as the earlier example suggests, initiate rule changes that involve movement toward generality. But prospects for agreement on constitutional generality must be distinguished categorically from unilateral behavior that would eschew opportunities for discrimination against members of existing minorities. Unconstrained majoritarian politics cannot be expected to produce results as if generality constraints are present when they are not. The constitutional rules within which majority voting rules operate assume critical importance. Subsequent chapters will examine specific applications of the analysis and will point toward specific changes that will, indeed, make majoritarian democracy, as constitutionally constrained, work more effectively.

PART THREE
Application

Introduction

As noted at the beginning of Chapter 2, we have considered it necessary to engage in "ideal theory" in order to establish the analytical foundations for the book's whole enterprise. We make no apologies for the use of the highly stylized, grossly simplified, and extremely abstracted models that have informed the preceding four chapters. We have sought to secure a *generalized* understanding of the generality principle before plunging into the complexities that any effort at application must introduce.

With Chapter 6, however, we move, perhaps abruptly, beyond reductionist exercises. In this and the following chapters in Part Three, we discuss familiar subject matters: externality, regulation, taxation, deficits, public goods, transfers, social insurance, and federalism. These policy-relevant categories of modern political economy offer the menu for application of the normative analysis of Part Two.

As the separate treatments will make clear, difficulties emerge in each case if we expect application of the generality norm to yield clear and unambiguous directions for specific constitutional change. As we note on several occasions, however, generality or nondiscrimination can offer criteria that allow proposed or observed political actions to be evaluated positively or negatively, without any satisfactory definitional determination of some idealized end point for politics. Recall that our subtitle is "Toward Nondiscriminatory Democracy."

6   Generality and externality

Life in a community is characterized by a variety of relationships with one's fellow community members. In a small community, these relationships may be entirely informal. Trading partners and neighbors may acknowledge mutual spheres of influence and trust which are understood only by the participants. Casual acquaintances may similarly acknowledge reciprocal duties of courtesy, assistance, and distance. Strangers may also interact within fairly well understood, if limited, rules of conduct. In a larger community, many of these informal relationships are formalized as law and regulation, and the somewhat less discerning, but stronger, sanctions of the village constabulary or state police replace those of neighborly disapproval and vendetta.

Although life within a community takes place within a complex web of rules and regulations, it is generally acknowledged to be superior to the life of a solitary unaffiliated person, a hermit, who escapes from the various rules governing life in a community. A community offers numerous opportunities for realizing increased personal wealth derived from trade among specialized producers as well as richer opportunities for consumption, fellowship, and education. These advantages evidently more than compensate individuals for the various formal and informal restrictions of life in a community.

Although adhering to the various rules and regulations associated with life within a community is clearly a burden for most individuals, the origins of many of those rules is based on mutual advantage. That is to say, many of a community's formal and informal regulations are not simply an unfortunate cost of life within a community, but rather a significant part of the reason why life in a community can be advantageous. Without at least some minimal formal and informal rules governing personal conduct, each person would find himself more adversely affected by the actions of fellow community residents than he would find himself advantaged by his own liberation from community rules. The realization of mutual advantages from coordinating and restricting personal behavior is, of course, one basis of the contractarian theory of the social contract.

Many of these mutually beneficial formal and informal rules of conduct address what economists call externality problems. Externality problems share the characteristic that persons are able to engage in activities which affect the welfare of other members of the community at large. To the extent that persons are unrestricted in their conduct, and free to ignore the effects of that conduct on other persons, it is clear that the overall result may be deficient from the point of view of all affected persons. In many of these cases, it will be possible for all persons to benefit from rules that circumscribe conduct which imposes costs on others and from rules that encourage conduct which confers benefits on others. As developed later, this is perhaps clearest in cases in which the external effects are reciprocal – that is, cases in which every person in the community both engages in and is affected by the conduct which generates external costs or benefits.

An important example of a reciprocal externality problem occurs in settings where several persons are able to use a common resource of limited productivity. In such cases, each person's use of the communal resource reduces the productivity of the resource for others with similar use rights. Each person's use of a communal water source, wood lot, or communal grazing area somewhat reduces the services that others may secure from those resources. Because each user may ignore the effects of his own actions on fellow users, unrestricted usage of such communal resources often leads to more intensive usage than that which maximizes useful output from the communal resource. The overgrazed and under-tended communal pasture is the well-known consequence of the "tragedy of the commons." To the extent that any increase in desired output from a common resource can be shared by all who use that resource, all such persons would benefit from rules which appropriately control the overall usage of common resources.

A variety of collective management devices could be adopted which can assure that relevant output is maximized (Ostrom, 1990; Cornes and Sandler, 1996). For example, "tragedies of the commons" can often be avoided by formally or informally partitioning the common resource into separate parcels controlled by a family or single individual (Demsetz, 1967). Nearly all of the productive effects of property rights systems can be analyzed as solutions to various externalities and commons problems. The particular methods used to ameliorate externality and commons problems are not of direct relevance for our present analysis, but the manner in which those methods are applied is of direct concern.

Insofar as resolving externality problems is accepted as a significant responsibility of a postconstitutional state, the causal basis of any externality or commons problems that might potentially be resolved is not technological but rather legal and cultural. Externality problems occur because current use-rights assignments, regulations, and sanctions fail to provide incentives that allow Pareto-efficient outcomes to emerge. Thus, in a postconstitutional setting, externality problems are properly considered to be instances of political failure rather than market failure. It is for this reason that the generality principle has a role to play in improving formal property rights systems and other mechanisms used to regulate externality generating conduct within every political community.

A. A digression on the active and passive management of the commons

As developed in Chapter 1, modern civil law has a constitutional character which essentially removes many resource allocation problems from the agenda of day-to-day majoritarian politics. In this, civil law has political properties similar to the generality principle in that it usefully restricts what might be placed on the political agenda. Other less permanent and passive management methods are, of course, also used to resolve externality problems. National resources may be managed actively as when a government bureaucracy harvests, holds, or sells timber and mining rights in a national forest. Or resources may be passively managed, as when transferable property rights are established over tracts of forest that allow individuals and firms to transact without active government oversight. Indeed, the collective management of resources within the geographic confines of a particular polity may be said to be unavoidable in a postconstitutional government given responsibility for resolving externality problems. However, there are a broad array of management methods that might be relied upon, and there are significant political efficiency differences between active and passive management methods that parallel those associated with the generality and uniformity with which such regulations may be promulgated and enforced.

The political efficiency advantage of using more permanent and passive methods is based on the likely responses that would follow from policies over which government decision makers have little discretion. The potential effects of political entrepreneurship become more limited as more permanent and passive management methods are adopted because such policies allow policymakers less discretion to amend existing policies or create new ones. Political entrepreneurs will be inclined to make smaller investment in forming new political coalitions, and consequently majoritarian cycles would tend to be less frequent.[1] This argument is perhaps clearest in the extreme case. If use rights to resources are permanently meted out in divisible parcels, future access to them is not restricted by one's influence at court or ability to assemble a majority coalition. Once *permanent* use rights are assigned, there is no possibility of effective political influence. And efforts to change permanent property entitlements are necessarily futile. Rational coalition builders and rent seekers clearly will not participate in the political influence game in areas governed by more or less permanent user-rights assignments.[2]

However, there is a fundamental problem with universally applying such durable passive management solutions. The efficiency of static management systems tends to change through time as technology, climate, population, and economic development change in unexpected ways. Consequently, every permanent assignment of user rights, or regulatory regime, is potentially inefficient. Fundamental limitations of human knowledge imply that there is a tradeoff between political cost savings of durability and the efficiency of the resource outcomes that emerge in the very long run. To ameliorate problems associated with durability, most polities have procedures for amending property law through time as circumstances change. The intermediate arrangements that we observe in the United States allow occasional amendments of use-rights assignments as political and economic circumstances change. Obviously, all amendments and extensions to existing law are consequences of political decision making.

It is clear that divisibility and tradability of rights reduce the need for revision of assignments. Voluntary exchange can in this case generate a more efficient allocation of resources than in settings with more restricted or indivisible bundles of ownership rights. However, even very tradable and divisible use rights may be inefficiently allocated in the sense that substantial transactions costs may rule out otherwise mutually beneficial Coase-like exchanges among affected parties. Transactions costs are more significant obstacles for large-number transactions in markets than in politics because market transactions must be completely voluntary. In cases in which there are significant multilateral externalities or obsolete legal impediments, typical of many environmental problems, active political intervention can often benefit the average citizen in settings where ordinary market transactions can not.

Because political decision making is unavoidable, the generality principle remains a possible means of improving majoritarian efforts to ameliorate externality problems even in polities which rely extensively upon private property rights to address resource allocation problems. In more pro-active democratic settings, the role of the generality principle will naturally tend to be greater, insofar as policymakers have greater discretion. In either case, any segmentation of users or alternative uses creates the possibility of off-diagonal majoritarian cycles, and elicits rent-seeking investments by those who may benefit or be harmed by differential treatment.

B. Illustrations from environmental regulation

One policy area in which public management has become significantly more active in recent years is environmental law. A number of factors have contributed to the growth of the modern body of environmental law. Population densities, and thereby externality production and intensities, have increased through time. Public sensibilities toward environmental matters have increased with rising income and the cumulative educational efforts of green groups. Economic rent seeking via environmental law has also increased, as, for example, chemical companies learn to lobby to secure bans on competitor's products. The environmental services industry lobbies for more stringent controls as a means of expanding the "demand" for its services. As environmental political equilibria shift, environmental regulations are amended (Congleton, 1996).

The environmental laws that governments have enacted over the years are sometimes in accord with generality and sometimes conflict with generality. Two examples from early American colonial history can serve as illustrations. In 1657, the burgomasters of New Amsterdam issued an ordinance prescribing that the streets be kept clean and that *all* rubbish and filth be deposited at certain designated places (Sopper, 1966). Generality is satisfied here insofar as all refuse is treated in the same manner irrespective of user or origin. In contrast, in 1681, William Penn, in his ordinance for the disposal of lands, required that *new* land owners leave an acre of forest standing for every five acres cleared (Meyer, 1966). Here, generality is violated because the law treats current and future landowners differently.

The arbitrariness of most segmentations of users creates natural avenues for rent seeking within any polity and a multiplicity of cleavage points for majority coalitions. For example, consider the many nongeneral methods by which a local highway congestion problem might be ameliorated. One might ban the use of dark gray automobiles on public highways during morning and evening rush hours simply because there are so many of them, or because they are more difficult to see than more brightly colored cars and so are more accident prone. One could ban old, young, and/or male drivers for similar reasons. One could ban all trucks and/or large cars during peak hours because they take up more scarce highway space than smaller cars. One could discriminate by hair color, race, or by length of journey. There are many possible rationalizations for choosing a subclass of users to shoulder the main burden of solving the congestion problem. So many plausible arguments can be made for treating different individuals differently that, in the end, differential treatment is arbitrary and susceptible to manipulation and rationalization by organized interest groups. While it may be debated whether or not unequal treatment may occasionally improve public policy, the rent-seeking expenditures engendered by such policies always remain a source of political inefficiency.[3]

In modern environmental law, different sources of identical effluents are often subject to different regulations, as for example emission standards of new and old automobiles are subject to differential regulations. Pesticides and additives that have fundamentally similar health risks are often subject to quite different regulatory targets (Ames, Magaw, and Gold, 1987; Cropper, Evans, Berardi, Duela Soares, and Portnoy, 1992). Land-use restrictions imposed on similar parcels of land are also subject to a wide range of variation. These idiosyncratic polices open environmental law up to the machinations of majoritarian politics and special interest groups while increasing enforcement and adherence costs.

The analysis of the previous chapters implies that adherence to the generality principle is one method of reducing the political cost of creating environmental law. A general body of environmental law reduces incentives for rent seeking and moderates the variation in environmental policies associated with majoritarian electoral cycles. It is somehat surprising that, for all the attention given to analyzing and creating new environmental law, little attention has been paid to the uniformity of the resulting body of environmental law.

C. Rotating majorities and generality in the regulation of reciprocal externalities

It remains to be determined whether a legislature bound by the generality principle can resolve externality problems. Savings from reduced rent-seeking losses and greater stability in majoritarian outcomes may be offset by reductions in conventional efficiency. In some cases, the generality restriction may preclude solutions to externality problems. The following analysis suggests that some degree of reciprocity in effects may be necessary for the generality rule to yield Pareto-efficient results in the regulation of externality generating behavior. The analysis also suggests that generality may retain its appeal as a principle for collective management even in cases in which it functions imperfectly insofar as it reduces incentives to substitute active public management of resources for private management in areas where private management is more efficient.

Reciprocal externalities have the property that each externality generator's behavior affects the welfare of others engaged in more or less similar activities. Noise is produced by all who live within an apartment building, annoying smoke is produced by all in a room full of smokers, drivers generate congestion of highways by their simultaneous road usage. Most cases in which a common resource is overused involve reciprocal externalities in this sense. In such cases, the generality principle can achieve Pareto-efficient outcomes suggested by the symmetric examples explored in earlier chapters.

Bob

		Refrains	Generates Externality
Al		I	II
	Refrains	3, 3	1, 4
	Generates	III	IV
	Externality	4, 1	2, 2

Figure 6.1. Reciprocal and symmetric externality regulatory outcomes.

For example, consider the case in which two persons, call them *Al* and *Bob*, engage in an activity that imposes external costs on the other. Each can choose to engage in the activity or not. Each receives personal net benefits from his own activity but imposes significant costs on the other. In this case, the choice setting can be represented as a symmetric game that resembles the classic PD problem. Figure 6.1 summarizes the utility payoffs generated by the four essential behavioral combinations. At the Nash, or voluntary adjustment, equilibrium without regulation, each person engages in the externality generating activity at the level that maximizes his own private benefits. The lower right-hand cell on the diagonal emerges from the separate choices.

The effects of alternative regulatory regimes can also be represented with the same matrix. A regulatory regime shifts the solution from one cell to another. For example, a rule prohibiting Bob from engaging in the externality generating behavior effectively eliminates Column II from the feasible set, if it is rigorously enforced. Because Al's behavior is not affected by this rule, the outcome is, in this setting, Cell III. A substantial tax or user fee imposed on Bob, but not on Al, has the same effect, although in this case the right-hand column is not eliminated by law, but the payoffs for Bob are reduced to ones below those in the left-hand column.

Such discriminating policies are of practical interest because each party benefits if the other unilaterally refrains from the externality generating activity. The latter implies that if either has the authority to choose the social state, each would opt for a policy that yields an off-diagonal solution in which the individual in authority engages in the externality generating activity while requiring the other to refrain. The possibility of off-diagonal policies may cause considerable resources to be wasted in conflict for political power. Each has an incentive to resist such policies and to attempt to gain control. Majoritarian cycling leads to rotation between the off-diagonal cells.

If possible solutions are restricted by the generality principle, political power is less significant in the symmetric case. Both individuals would choose Cell I, which is Pareto efficient. Here, neither engages in the externality generating activity. Complete symmetry in the payoffs implies consensus about the relative merits of alternative policies allowed by the generality rule. This clearly reduces conflict over political power and increases the legitimacy of the results of political choices in so far as policy outcomes reflect consensus rather than arbitrary power.

The logic of this analysis applies to all cases in which the rank order of payoffs is symmetric. This is often the case when a common resource is an input into several different production processes and there is some fixed capital. The *absolute* value of payoffs may differ substantially among the parties without changing the incentives for the exercise of political power with the generality rule. So long as the relative payoffs to large-scale and small-scale users of a commons, as might be the case for commercial and sport fisherman fishing in the same lake, are *ordinally equivalent* along the diagonal, each prefers the same access level under generality.

D. Rotating majorities and generality in the collectivization of nonreciprocal externalities

Application of the generality principle to the regulation of externalities becomes problematic even under reciprocal externalities in cases in which significant asymmetries exist among the participants. For example, if the rank order of payoffs along the diagonal differs among players, the players will disagree about the proper stringency of restrictions on externality generating behavior even if constrained by the generality principle. (Recall our discussion of the publicness analogy to this model in Chapter 3.) In such cases adherence to the generality principle will yield different results according to which coalition is in power. A generality rule does not fully end conflict over political power, but it does moderate such conflict because on-diagonal outcomes are necessarily less exploitative in the sense that any on-diagonal outcome is dominated by off-diagonal payoffs for any coalition in authority.

A considerably less tractable problem arises in settings in which the externality is not reciprocal in the sense that one person's or group's activities affect some other's welfare, but not vice versa. In such cases, application of the generality principle when the activity is collectivized may generate perverse results.

To see this, again using the two-person model for wider purpose, suppose that Al gains no personal advantage from the externality generating activity but, instead, considers the activity to involve a net cost. By contrast, Bob does benefit from his own behavior in the activity in question while he suffers potential loss from the activity of the other person. In this setting, the unregulated, or uncollectivized, Nash solution entails Al refraining from and Bob undertaking the activity in question. For a familiar example, think of Bob as a smoker and Al as a nonsmoker who both share a closed space. The Nash or voluntary equilibrium may be Pareto optimal, (Cell II of Figure 6.2), but, nonetheless, Al may think that he could benefit if the externality generating activity could be brought under public (collective) authority.

Bob

		Refrains	Generates Externality
Al		I	II
	Refrains	4, 2	3, 4
	Generates Externality	III 2, 1	IV 1, 3

Figure 6.2. Nonreciprocal externality regulatory outcomes.

If Al could write the regulations, he would enact rules that would yield Cell I, on the diagonal, where neither person engages in the activity. If Bob has the power to choose regulations, he will choose Cell II, the original voluntary Nash equilibrium. Both these outcomes are Pareto optimal, so there may be no mutuality of advantage in moving this externality generating activity into the sphere of active political management. However, collectivization (politicization) of the activity under majority rule combined with adherence to the generality rule in this case may yield Pareto-suboptimal results. A generality rule would allow only policy choices along the diagonal. This rule would not affect Al's desired outcome (Cell I), but it does affect Bob's (Cell II). If constrained by the generality principle and he were in authority, Bob would choose Cell IV, *where each person is forced to engage in the externality generating activity*. This cell is Pareto dominated by the original Nash equilibrium.[4] Both parties would prefer the voluntaristic, or noncollectivized, solution to that which would be enforced if Bob were in authority. Here, politicization with generality may generate either Pareto-optimal results or Pareto-inferior results according to which party has the power to make and enforce regulations.

This example seems bizarre only because of the failure to distinguish between some initial or separated decision to collectivize or politicize an interaction among persons and the decision that might be made to regulate the activity of separate persons once the interaction is collectivized. In the setting depicted in the two-person, two-action matrix of Figure 6.2, there is no "logic of collective action" in the ordinary sense, because there is no mutuality of gain promised from any shift away from the fully voluntaristic Nash equilibrium (Cell II). Collectivization finds its legitimacy in some promised mutuality of gain for all interacting parties.

As the example suggests, however, collectivization offers one means through which the preferences of one set of interacting parties may be imposed on the other. If, in the example, Al thinks that he, or his group, can remain in positions of political authority, collectivization of the activity (e.g., smoking) allows Bob to be coerced to satisfy Al's preferences – and with the accompanying argument that the generality norm is not thereby violated. In 1919, the prohibitionists did not violate the generality norm: they prohibited the production, sale, and consumption of alcohol for *all*. When the nonprohibitionists coalition attained political authority in 1932, it did not seek to apply the generality principle under collectivization by forcing alcohol on everyone. Instead, this coalition decollectivized the activities, at least in part. One of the major advantages of allowing the organization of activities to remain in the noncollectivized sector is that persons and groups may behave differently; there is no normative argument to the effect that all persons should behave similarly.

E. Generality and the evolution of property rights

In a dynamic setting, the issue of interest is whether the generality principle encourages beneficial amendments to property rights assignments in the long run. That is to say, would groups seeking to change use-rights assignments be more interested in efficiency-increasing than in efficiency-decreasing revisions of use rights if restricted by a generality principle? This section demonstrates that even in cases in which ordinary policy efficiency is not found along the diagonal, the generality principle often retains a constitutional appeal.

Some sense of the dynamic efficiency of the generality principle may be obtained by analyzing decisions to switch from voluntary to active public management – that is, from private to communal use-rights systems. Proper incentives to motivate the change are clearly evidenced for the reciprocal externality class that yields a game with payoffs similar to those of the symmetric PD game. Here there exists, of course, the standard "logic of collective action."

In the absence of some sort of restriction on externality generating behavior, both Al and Bob engage in the activity, and each realizes a payoff lower than that which would be possible under symmetrical behavior involving inaction. At this point, each has an incentive to lobby for new rules because new rules potentially would allow each to realize the preferred outcome.

Incentives to lobby for government to take active responsibility for managing resources are clear if the utility indicators are assumed for purposes of illustration to characterize cardinal, as well as ordinal, payoffs. Under unconstrained collectivization with cyclic majorities, both off-diagonal possibilities are more or less equally likely. In the numerical example of Figure 6.3 (which duplicates Figure 6.1), each expected payoff is $.5(1) + .5(4) = 2.5$ if the activity is turned over to the government, choices for which are made by a majority coalition. Interpreted as von Neumann–Morgenstern expected utilities, the expected payoff for each player is larger than that at the Nash equilibrium $(2.5 > 2)$, and each would favor government intervention.[5] In the limit, each would be willing to pay up to a half unit of output to change from voluntary to collective management.

But the returns to active collectivization are even greater under the application of the generality principle. Under generality, neither party will engage in the externality generating activity even if in the decisive majority, thereby ensuring each person a payoff of three *with certainty*. Thus, each person would be willing to pay up to one unit

Bob

	Refrains	Generates Externality
Al	I	II
Refrains	3, 3	1, 4
Generates	III	IV
Externality	4, 1	2, 2

Figure 6.3. Externality dilemma.

Bob

	Refrains	Generates Externality
Al	I	II
Refrains	4, 2	3, 4
Generates	III	IV
Externality	2, 1	1, 3

Figure 6.4. Technological change and incentives to relinquish public management.

of output to achieve such results. The greater efficiency of generality in such a case warrants greater political investments that can overcome greater institutional frictions.

A similar result holds for the case in which technological change reduces the need for active intervention. This can be demonstrated with reference to the problematic nonreciprocal externality game examined previously. Figure 6.4 (which duplicates Figure 6.2) reproduces those payoffs. In a government bound by the generality rule, each party receives a two-and-one-half unit expected payoff from active management by rotating coalitions (between the solutions in Cells I and IV). By comparison, the voluntary adjustment solution (Cell II) involves a payoff of three for one party and four for the other. Risk neutral players would agree to a constitutional decollectivization, that is, to privatization of the activity. Risk averse players would pay a bit more than this to avoid uncertain electoral cycles.

The consensus for privatization disappears if political outcomes are not constrained by the generality principle. In the unconstrained case, changes in the ruling coalition again lead to policy changes. Note that in this case, the policy outcomes oscillate between the two top cells of the matrix rather than along the diagonal. In the numerical example, the expected payoffs from this rotation are three-and-one-half and three, for Al and Bob, respectively. Bob would be willing to pay to move to privatization, but Al benefits from the active collective management, even under anticipated majoritarian rotation.

F. The existence of political inefficiency

Under a variety of circumstances, the efficiency of the generality principle will lead many to favor its implementation, and we should observe generality as an active element of governance simply because it often benefits all parties in a dynamic world. We do observe a considerable amount of general legislation: more generality than one might think likely in a setting in which legislation is formally unconstrained (Shepsle, 1981). (For example, see our analysis of public retirement programs as discussed in Chapter 11.) This observation suggests that the dynamic argument as outlined in the previous section has an empirical basis. However, the generality principle is often violated in the regulation of externalities. Nor are departures from generality limited to cases in which nongeneral treatments enhance efficiency.

What is the critical difference? In cases in which only a subset of the population of voters or potential interest groups may influence or control policy, the relatively potent groups will prefer narrow-to-broad programs because they realize above-average benefits while bearing average or below-average program costs. So long as a significant portion of the relevant population of voters remains outside politically effective groups because of differences in organization or voting costs, interest groups may transfer wealth from the ineffective groups to themselves.

To see this, consider the case in which the burden of internalizing an externality may be shifted among three groups: A, B, and C, where C is the ineffective group. Suppose that A and B roughly alternate in their control of the policy, whereas Group C never gains control. Figure 6.5 depicts payoffs that typical members of Groups A, B, and C realize from the differential policies that may be adopted. As in the previous figures, the payoffs do not represent the simultaneous choices of the traditional PD game but rather the payoffs associated with the use of discriminatory and nondiscriminatory policy tools to deal with externality problems. The discriminatory tool is assumed to be inferior to the general tool for the purposes of policy. Consequently, the highest total payoff occurs when the general policy is applied, and the lowest payoff occurs when the discriminatory tool is uniformly applied to all parties outside the dominant coalition. The discriminatory policy tool allows a group to shift the burden

Group *B*

	Uses General Policy Tool	Uses Discriminatory Tool on *A* and *C*
Group *A* Uses General Policy Tool	I (3, 3, 3)	II (1, 4, 1)
Uses Discriminatory Tool on *B* and *C*	III (4, 1, 1)	IV --

Figure 6.5. Payoffs from discriminatory policy.

of internalizing an externality to members of the other groups. In any single round of the game, each potential ruling coalition benefits most if it uses a discriminatory policy (4 > 3). For example, the ruling coalition might mandate that nonmembers plant and maintain attractive gardens along sidewalks bordering their properties but exempt the ruling coalition because of its "special" circumstances.

In the setting analyzed here, where two of three groups effectively rotate collective authority between themselves, there may or may not be sufficient differential values between discriminatory and nondiscriminatory payoffs to cause these groups to support the generality principle, which would enforce nondiscrimination. Under such a rule, these groups would not be able to discriminate against the ineffective group, *C* in the example here, but each group would avoid unfavorable discrimination in out-of-authority situations.

If the ineffective, or continually exploited, group is large, relative to the membership of the two rotating effective groups, we should not expect that the latter would support application of the generality rule. In this case, the burden of discriminatory policy would fall disproportionately on the noneffective group to the benefit of the effective groups, one of which is presumed to be in authority in all periods. Reductions in the externality generating activities of a large number of nonmembers allow relatively large reductions in aggregate externality levels to be secured at little or no cost to the privileged group. Consequently, the returns to members of politically effective groups may be substantial insofar as they have unusually strong aversions to the externality or realize significant pecuniary advantage from efforts to curtail or control the activity in question. Thus nongeneral policies may continue to find political support in practice despite significant effects on average payoffs.

G. Intergenerational and sequential externalities

Although our analysis has implicitly been aimed at long-term solutions to ongoing externality problems, we have not explicitly used the language or models of inter-generational analyses or indeed dealt explicitly with what might more generally be called *sequential externalities* – externalities that are not simultaneous but, rather, occur sequentially through time. The situation faced by successive and overlapping generations of individuals is sufficiently similar in many cases, that one can imagine all parties in all generations reaching agreements along the lines discussed throughout our book. For example, in the case of fundamental property institutions, the opportunity to exchange rights remains useful at every point in time for all living persons insofar as mutual gains to trade can be realized. In other cases, the order of play may not be known or even predetermined, and every player may, in effect, face a similar and symmetric choice about whether to play the game at every instant. The finite sequential PD game is well-known to have properties that largely parallel those of the simple unrepeated game. In such cases, sequential externality and commons problems can be analyzed largely within a steady-state or atemporal framework similar to that previously developed.

In cases in which there is a sufficient commonality of interests among individuals through time or sufficient overlap of interests, a single set of constitutional rules, which includes the generality principle, can be in the interest of every possible successive population of voters. In such cases, the constitution adopted may be said to be subgame perfect in the sense that a single stable set of rules continues to be in the interest of each successive population of voters. In such circumstances, the sequential nature of the problem and/or the finite time periods in which particular individuals participate in and are affected by political choices can be neglected without significant cost in order to simplify analysis and facilitate exposition.

In other settings, sequential elements of the problem may be expected to undermine a constitutional consensus that mandates general and uniform treatment across generations. For example, in some cases in which the "order of play" is predetermined and known before hand, as is necessarily the case in intergenerational games, the political and economic advantage of the first movers can be significant. This is well-known for the case of entry in markets, as in the Stackelberg model of duopoly. In intergenerational political economy games, the advantage of early generations can be even greater than in the classic Stackelberg model of sequential entry into private markets because subsequent players may not be able to affect the payoffs of the first movers. For example, if generation two or three does not overlap with generation one, they cannot materially affect generation one, whether for good or ill. The technological innovations of generation one can be shared or withheld from succesive generation three, but the innovations of generation three clearly cannot be shared with generation one. The arrow of time often implies similar asymmetries in many long-term externality problems. Earlier generations often can substantially affect future generations, but not vice versa.

To take an extreme example of continuing hypothetical interest, suppose that generation one completely destroys some stock of a natural resource, (e.g., petroleum, buffalo hides, regional aquifers, or blue skys) and generation two cannot reciprocate. From behind a veil of ignorance, one can easily imagine cases in which all persons in every generation would agree to a generality rule that would give each person an equal claim on the resource in question or guarantee some minimal tradable endowment in the resource. But it is equally clear that, in practice, each generation would have an incentive (in the absence of sufficiently dynastic ethical systems or utility functions) to violate any general agreement reached and to overutilize the resource in question. Insofar as the power to amend a constitution necessarily rests with the living, even constitutionally mandated generality in such policy areas is not politically feasible.

Note that application of the generality principle to this last intergenerational problem differs in several respects from the politically based argument developed previously. Generality in this case cannot be based on increased political efficiency in the sense emphasized throughout this volume because the affected current and future individuals cannot directly negotiate, agree, and codify political self-restraint in real time. Consequently, the symmetry induced by rotating majorities is absent. Moreover, intergenerational generality does not, in this instance, benefit the politically active parties. It, therefore, lacks the continuing political appeal that, at least potentially, ensures the durability of the generality rule in most of our previous examples. Every generation would benefit by taking more than "its share" of the resource in question. (Also, see Chapter 9.)

Fortunately relatively few resources are effectively destroyed on use. Most metals and plastics can be reclaimed and recycled. Most local landscapes can be returned to attractive contours, and most local ecosystems are fairly robust in that they can largely regenerate themselves within a few decades. (Much of the forestland in the eastern United States and in western Europe was farmland in previous centuries.) Moreover, economic growth, to the extent that it is acknowledged to take place, offsets increased scarcity in some resource areas with reduced scarcity elsewhere. In particular, manufactured goods, including capital and knowledge, tend to increase with economic growth. To the extent that resources consumed by manufacture are mainly valued as *inputs* into a production process (i.e., valued as means rather than ends), numerous possibilities for substitution often remain. Many of these substitutes will become relatively cheaper through time as knowlege and skill advance. Thus, the intergenerational problem is not generally as stark as the example seems to indicate, although specific problematic cases may still be important.

H. Conclusion: Externalities and political failure

Constitutional solutions tend to be long-term solutions. In a static world, one could, in principle, contrive permanent property rights and regulatory mechanisms to deal with most externality problems while minimizing rent-seeking activities. For example, active collective management might be restricted to activities in which on-diagonal solutions are Pareto optimal, as argued in Chapter 5. Commons and externality problems may be avoided elsewhere by creating tradable use rights secured with penalties and torts administered in an efficient judicial system. Voluntary exchange between individuals or groups of individuals, possibly coordinated by regional government organizations, could maximize the value of outputs from those resources. Illegitimate use of resources could be punished via ordinary civil or criminal law. However, in cases in which technological or other changes affect the payoffs of externality generating activities or create new unanticipated possibilities, the ideal pattern, range, and domain of use rights change through time, often in ways that cannot be anticipated. So long as political decisions have to be reached on such matters, there remains an important role for the generality principle as a guide to policy formation.

Inefficient property laws or inefficient regulations that we observe in a democracy are largely equilibrium outcomes of a majoritarian politics. The analysis developed in this chapter suggests that a majoritarian democracy unconstrained by the generality principle is very likely to adopt inefficient discriminatory regulatory methods. Here, as in other policy areas, the generality principle improves the performance of majoritarian decision making by reducing the likelihood of discriminatory policies and thereby reducing the magnitude of resources consumed by political conflict.

7 Market restriction and the generality norm

In this chapter we analyze the generality norm as it might act to constrain political interferences with trade or exchange, whether such interferences are promotive or restrictive in purpose and whether trade is exclusively among citizens (internal or domestic) or between citizens and persons or firms in other political jurisdictions (external or foreign).

The thrust of the argument is dramatic in its demonstration that *any* interference with market allocation that is exclusively motivated by political purpose must reflect a violation of the generality norm. This result, in its turn, implies that the precise decision rule for making political choices becomes irrelevant if a constitutional requirement for generality is in place. Majoritarian politics is, of course, systemically organized to produce departures from generality in treatment among groups, but if *all* departures from generality are prohibited by effective constitutional constraint, majority decision rules operate much as alternative rules in maintaining emergent market allocation. The economists' normative argument in support of the superior efficiency of resource allocation generated in nonpoliticized markets is reinforced by the argument concerning the political efficacy of the generality norm. This norm, if operative as a constitutional constraint, ensures that the "all-encompassing interest," reflected in the maximal value of produce, as evaluated by the preferences of participants and subject to the transfer proviso discussed later, will be chosen as preferred by any coalition in a position of collective authority. In effect, the constitutionalization of generality in treatment indirectly amounts to the constitutionalization of market allocation in settings in which public goods and externalities are not present. This conclusion remains applicable even in those settings in which income–wealth transfers, motivated exclusively by distributional considerations, may be implemented through collective auspices. (See the discussion in Chapters 8 and 10.) Any such transfer process will, of course, exert some incentive effects. The aggregate value of goods and services produced will be maximized by market allocation, subject to the stipulated transfer scheme. Our focus in this chapter is on the effects of the generality requirement on the proclivity of political coalitions to interfere in particular markets.

A. Political interferences with internal trade

We observe modern democracies intervening in the liberties of persons and groups within the polity to make voluntary exchanges among themselves. Governments, everywhere, do more than carry out protective state functions; they go beyond enforcing rights to property and contracts. In almost all cases, however, the politicized interferences that we observe are justified rhetorically through some argument to the effect that interests of persons and groups beyond those directly impacted are promoted. This or that action is to be politically promoted, through regulation, tax exemption, or

76

subsidies, because it allegedly generates external or spillover benefits on others than those directly involved in the transactions. This or that industry or product category is to be politically restricted because extended production–consumption involves alleged negative externalities. In this section, we shall limit discussion to those possible interferences with domestic trade that *cannot* be justified, on any honest evaluation, on the basis of either externality or public goods arguments.

We acknowledge, as we must, that the distinction between those situations in which externality and public goods elements provide legitimate bases for politicization and those in which claims about the existence of such elements remain empty is difficult to make, and especially in the sometimes obscurantist rhetoric of ordinary politics. We are, in a sense, taking the easy way out here by concentrating attention on those situations in which politicized interferences occur in the absence of any legitimate general welfare enhancing claims.

The discussion of the elementary political logic of particularized trade promotion or restriction will be postponed until Section B, in application to trade between citizens and foreigners. With respect to domestic trade, defined inclusively to refer to the production and exchange of goods and services at all levels of usage and among both persons and firms, we want first to emphasize the point made earlier. The basic model of majoritarian politics, as developed in the first five chapters of this book, does not appear to be descriptive of the reality that we have historically observed. The generality principle that we have placed at center stage as the criterion for nondiscriminatory politics seems to have been operative, at least in part and indirectly. Majority coalitions have been reluctant, perhaps surprisingly so, to interfere in piecemeal fashion with liberties of domestic exchange on the basis of explicit promotion of the interests of coalition members, as such. Modern democracy does not behave comparably to Tudor England by granting private monopoly rights to producers–sellers of playing cards and gaming tables.

We do observe some particular exceptions to the principle of noninterference, even in situations in which there are no clearly claimed externality arguments. In the United States, markets for agricultural goods are rarely observed to be free of politicized restrictions, aimed to increase profits (rents) for producer groups (tobacco, sugar, peanuts, cotton, and milk). These market restrictions are widely recognized, however, to be exceptions rather than to represent the majoritarian norm, which seems to remain one of noninterference.

Critics may suggest that the same results as overt market restrictions may be accomplished by political manipulation of the tax code, which is omnipresent. However, the very fact that such an indirect means of differential treatment is deemed to be politically necessary suggests that overt differentiation through the political process is, somehow, out of bounds.

Quite apart from the fact that monopoly rights are not explicitly granted, modern democracies do not enact legislation that allows for the enforcement of contracts among members of potential industry-wide cartels. Indeed the whole structure of legislation aimed to enforce competition, summarized under the rubric "anti-trust laws" in the United States, can be interpreted as an application of the generality precept. By thinking of these laws (and the derivative institutions designed for their implementation) as effectively constitutional in nature, the inclusive rules of the political–economic game embody equality in treatment as among all potential entrants into and exit from any productive category. Persons are thereby assured that political majorities will not discriminate, either positively or negatively, among economically classified groups on the basis of coalition membership or electoral success or failure. Further, persons are assured that the protective legal umbrella, itself subject to political manipulation, will not be extended to allow the enforcement of privately motivated contracts in restraint of trade.

The level of economic well-being would be dramatically lower in a political regime that failed to respect the generality norm in the indirect sense outlined. Imagine the prospects that would face an investor in a setting in which expected rates of return depended largely on membership in a successful majority coalition. Not only would the variance among expected rates of return for different investments be larger because of the inclusion of an estimate for political success or failure, but, also, success or failure in this respect would, itself, be implemented by interventions that would, in themselves, be value reducing. The promotion of the interests of one industry, or coalition of industries, can only be accomplished at the expense of others. In the process, there may be a transfer of economic value, but, perhaps, more importantly, potential value will be destroyed. To the extent that direct interference with liberty of exchange is kept out of bounds for the workings of ordinary politics, any such destruction of potential value is prevented while political risk on investment is reduced.

B. Political interferences in external trade

At century's end, violations of the generality principle that take the form of explicitly discriminatory treatment of economically distinguishable groups (classified by industry or product category) are not, perhaps, objects of major concern, at least in the United States. Much more serious issues emerge, however, for politically orchestrated interferences with freedom of external markets, where trade takes place between citizens or domestic organizations (firms) and foreigners, either individuals or organizations. There seems to be little or no carryover of the generality norm against interferences in external trade, and proponents of interference apparently confront no pressures that dictate presentation of supporting argument in a rhetoric of public interest.

The elementary logic of politicized interferences with markets is, of course, identical for both domestic (internal) and foreign (external) settings. In any of the roles as specialized producer, whether as employee, executive, stockholder, or creditor, persons have an economic interest in restricting industry output below competitive levels in order to generate positive profits, even if, in many cases, such profits are recognized to be transitory. In any ordering of alternative regimes, producers (using this term inclusively to cover all who share interests in a single activity) will ideally prefer that their own industry be monopolized (cartelized) under governmental protection, whereas *all other* industries are open to the forces of market competition. Such a differentially protected regime is preferred because any producer is, at the same time, a nonspecialized consumer who purchases, for use as inputs or as end items, goods from others. And, clearly, the producer's interest as purchaser–user is to face prices that are as low as possible in all markets other than his own. Ideally, therefore, any producer group seeks discriminatory protection of its own industry while simultaneously opposing protection for all other industries. Such a result would be forthcoming, however, only if, somehow, political authority is captured or controlled by the single producer group.

Realistically, any industry, or its representative, that seeks protective governmental action must recognize that it can probably succeed only as a partner in a coalition of producer groups, each one of which expects to secure protection of its own market. The regime that might seem politically practicable, involving a coalition of separate producer groups, will be less profitable to any member group than the idealized regime that protects only the single market.

How large must a coalition be in order to be ensured of political success? If democratic representation is organized exclusively on the basis of industry groups, a response would be straightforward. An effective coalition would require a majority of constituents to be included, and, hence, cartel or monopoly protection would be extended to the number of industries required to make up such a majority. If there are 100 producer groups, each with roughly the same number of potential beneficiaries, a successful political coalition would involve more than 50 of these groups. Market protection would be extended to cover somewhat more than one-half of the economic activity of the polity. Any effort to extend restrictions over only a minority of industries would fail politically because a majority of constituents would find their interests, as ultimate consumers, damaged by such action.

We should note, however, that precisely because a substantial coalition is necessary for political success, the preferred degree of market restriction would be well below that measured by the ideal restriction for the single industry that might, somehow, secure unique protection. (For detailed analysis on this and other points see Buchanan and Lee, 1991.) Hence, the larger the size of the coalition, the less the departure would be from the competitive allocation in the economy.

The basis for legislative representation is not exclusively, or even primarily, industrial or by product or resource categories. Hence, the exemplified model used in the argument previously discussed must be qualified. A producer group, which we call an *industry* (e.g., textiles), that seeks politically enforced restriction for its market may find that its members are widely scattered among the separate electoral districts represented in the legislature. To the extent that the correspondence between electoral districts and producer concentration by industry is attenuated, the formation of successful majority coalitions aimed at restricting foreign entry into domestic markets becomes more difficult. A legislator, who considers acting on behalf of localized producers, who seeks market restriction, must also reckon on the opposition of others in her constituency who are consumers–users, not only of the goods that are locally produced but also of the other goods that are included in the potential majoritarian coalition.

Despite the necessary qualifying arguments, however, there is sufficient concentration of producer groups by industry geographically or locationally to generate a delineation of legislative representation – notably in the United States Congress.

"Politics by interest" appears at its worst in discussions of restrictions on foreign imports into domestic markets. The logic of the stylized model sketched out earlier carries considerable explanatory weight in any evaluation of tariff history. (Early nineteenth-century American history, in particular, offers an example of the workings of the majoritarian democratic politics through which some members of the inclusive polity – citizens of the South and West – were exploited to the putative benefit of citizens of the North and East by the device of protective tariffs.)

We have not specifically discussed the natural coalition of producer interests that is defined by the distinction between domestic and foreign markets. Producers who sell their wares in domestic markets may seek to restrict market access by denying entry to foreign suppliers, either through prohibition or discriminatory tariffs and quotas. If they succeed, other producer interests who sell goods to foreigners must be damaged because, indirectly, these producers are necessarily consumers for the goods produced in the restricted markets. We must recognize, therefore, that, even if, say, tariff protection is extended at a uniform rate over all imports, such action clearly violates the generality precept because it discriminates overtly against those producing interests that seek only to enter exchanges in domestic markets or to sell to foreigners. And any such market restriction also discriminates against persons in their roles as consumers or final users of goods and services. Politically enforced market restriction that classifies goods by domestic or foreign origin generates off-diagonal outcomes, to revert to the matrix metaphor introduced earlier.

Again we should note, however, that political action may be judged against the generality criterion even if full satisfaction of the idealized constitutional norm is not met. A tariff that is imposed on all imports at a uniform rate is more general than a structure that imposes differential rates of duty. And any tariff, even on a single good, imposes the same rate on all quantities of that good and, hence, remains more general than an import quota that, effectively, levies zero rates on some units and prohibitive rates on other units of the same good. The predicted consequences are easy to outline. Motivation for wasteful rent-seeking investment varies inversely with the degree to which the generality criterion is satisfied. The relationship here may be applied usefully conversely, with perhaps some empirical content. The amount of rent seeking that can be observed to take place becomes a measure of the departure of policy from the generality norm.[1]

C. Application of a generality constraint

Consider a setting in which there exists a constitutional constraint against discriminatory political treatment as among separate economic interest groups. How would such a generality requirement affect the feasibility space of majoritarian coalitions? In getting at an answer here, we need to specify the model for analysis more fully.

As a first step, we may assume that all persons in the polity are, at the same time, both producers and consumers. That is to say, there are no pure consumers, whose economic interests are necessarily unidirectional. Assume, further, that all persons are nonspecialized as consumers but fully specialized as producers. This enables us to classify groups of persons by producing interests alone, although as indicated earlier, we take note of their accompanying interests as generalized consumers.

Suppose, now, that the natural coalition of producers of import substitutes seeks to secure the levy of a uniform tariff on all imported goods. Clearly, if this effort is successful, other economic interests are differentially damaged to the putative benefit of the favored producers of import substitutes. The generality norm is violated; the proposal would be unconstitutional because, by supposition, the generality constraint dictates that all interests, whether involved in producing for the domestic or foreign market, must be treated similarly. Generalization of the restriction on some markets might take the form of export subsidies to producers who sell to foreigners and cartelization of those who produce strictly for domestic markets. But what might be used as a signifier of satisfaction of the generality requirement here? What offsetting restrictions and/or promotions would meet the stylized generality constraint? What could possibly be analogous to the flat tax?

These questions can be answered only in an indirect manner. All producer groups would be treated in the same way if, when market restrictions are generally applied, there is *no* allocative change. Neither the pattern of resource usage nor the structure of input and output prices could change if the generality principle is indeed to be satisfied. Any change that results strictly from politically motivated efforts at market restriction or promotion must, itself, reflect the presence of some intended discriminatory impact. Those persons who shift resources must be induced to do so by the expectation of positive or negative rents.

Consider the tariff levied uniformly on all imported goods. Domestic production of these goods will increase as resources shift into the industries affected. Relatively, prices for imported goods increase; prices for other goods fall. Specialized producers in import-substitute industries find rents increased; specialized producers in other industries find rents decreased. The political action represented by the tariff discriminates in favor of some producers against others.

Elementary economic theory demonstrates that total value, as measured by the revealed preferences of all participants, in the economy is reduced by any strictly political interference with market allocation processes. (Recall that the model explicitly excludes externalities and public goods distortions.) But there is nothing in the political decision process, with any nonunanimity rule, that suggests economic value as a maximand. The implementation of a generality principle, through enforceable constitutional constraints that prohibit discriminatory impact, offers an alternative that may be indirectly effective. It seems possible that constitutional prohibitions against discriminatory treatment may secure support, whereas more specific prohibitions against any and all market restrictions might fail to do so.

In the stylized matrix illustrations introduced in Chapters 2 through 5, the critical distinction drawn was that between off-diagonal and on-diagonal positions, with only the second set meeting the generality or equal treatment requirement. The enforcement of generality reduces the size of the set of admissible alternatives for political–collective action, and a final choice among these alternatives, left for the workings of ordinary politics, depends on the particular rule that is in place for reaching final political decisions. In some abstracted sense, the several possible rules – single person, majority, unanimity, and others – seem likely to generate differing final outcomes.

In the application considered in this chapter, which involves political intervention into market allocation in the presumed absence of Pareto-relevant externalities and public goods, the generality constraint would again seem to be met by any position on an imagined diagonal, where all interests are treated equally or symmetrically. What is noteworthy in this application, however, is the dominance of a single position under any and all collective decision rules. Consider, quite simply, alternative proposals to restrict the output uniformly for *all* industries by, say, ten percent, twenty percent, and so on. Clearly, any such proposal would be dominated, for any decisive coalition, by embodying no restriction on *any* industry. That is to say, given a constitutional requirement of generality in treatment, any rule, whether dictating assent by a single person, a majority, or all participants, will, under the presumption that choosers are rational utility maximizers, generate the noninterference outcome, in which all interests are treated equally in the sense that no interests are either discouraged or encouraged by political action. The point may be made differently by stating that even if a single person, a small group, or a majority coalition possesses full authority to choose for the inclusive political community, an enforceable generality constraint should prevent economically advantageous discrimination on behalf of those with decision-making authority and against others outside the limits of this group. Any and all efforts to intervene in the market process, within the limits imposed by the generality constraint, could only prove costly to decision makers, as well as to all others in the polity.

This dominance of the noninterference outcome under all decision rules is not present in other applications of the generality constraint on political action. In the social insurance or welfare setting discussed in Chapter 11, in the public goods setting examined in Chapter 10, or in the externality setting treated in Chapter 6, the generality constraint eliminates off-diagonal outcomes, but differing decision rules may generate differing solutions from within this on-diagonal set. The reason for the difference between market intervention, as politically orchestrated, and political action in the other applications stems from the absence of any shared value in the former. The value that is produced by the operation of the market, in the absence of all publicness, defined inclusively and assumed here, is totally partitionable, as among separately identifiable interacting participants. The value that a person receives in the market process is not derived from a good or service that is simultaneously shared, and possibly valued, by another person. Nor is the value to the person an argument in the utility function of another person, at least in the formal analysis as stylized.

There is no need that separate persons come to an explicit agreement on the quantitative measure of that which provides value to any single person because this measure may differ as among persons. By contrast, in the other applications, an element of publicness is necessarily present. All members of the collective unit must share in a uniquely determinate outcome that may be valued differently for the sharers. Hence, the decision rule matters. In the idealized market, on the other hand, each person remains interested solely in maximizing the value that she is, personally, able to secure, given the parameters of interaction that include the endowments and preferences of others and the presence of the generality constraint that ensures against discriminatory political action. Each person is interested, therefore, in maximizing the value potential for the whole economy because only when this potential is maximized can her own value attain its highest level.

The argument for nonintervention in market allocation that emerges from application of the generalization principle offers an unconventional, and quite indirect, normative basis for the policy framework that is often summarized under the rubric of classical liberalism. Economists have long been frustrated at the failure of citizens to support the explicit objective of allocative efficiency. And they have remained unable to respond to the questions: "Why should I (any person) be interested in aggregate efficiency in resource usage? Is it not appropriate that my primary interest should be in the value that I may, individually, expect to secure, whether from participation in the market or in politics?"

Given the argument sketched out in this chapter, a possibly effective response might be as follows: "Indeed it is, but do you want to take part in politics that is necessarily discriminatory? And do you think that discriminatory politics will generate results that are personally beneficial? If you want to participate in politics that embodies generality in its treatment of all persons and all interests, you must acknowledge the desirability of constitutional constraints against discrimination – constraints that will, indirectly, maximize your expected value."

Appendix

Most favored nation clauses

We have discussed the generality principle, in its possible use as a constitutional constraint, as a means through which the discriminatory proclivities of domestic majoritarian politics might be brought under some control. Somewhat interestingly, we find that one version of the generality principle has been discussed widely and applied in international economic relations among separate countries, for quite different purposes than those that are aimed to curb the redistributional excesses of majority coalitions within countries. Most Favored Nation (MFN) clauses have been negotiated in international trade treaties, both bilaterally and multilaterally, for many years. These clauses specify that traders or exporters from a designated nation-state shall not be treated differently from traders from another nation-state when they seek entry into the market of the signatory state. These MFN clauses do not include stipulations as to allowable levels of tariff protection; instead they are aimed only at forestalling discriminatory treatment by origin.

Discrimination by country of origin among prospective traders who seek entry into domestic markets, with some sources being allowed entry while others are prohibited, or with differing sources confronted with differing rates of duty, would predictably create international conflict, whether cold, lukewarm, or hot. Further, incentives would be set up for international rent seeking that might take the form of unnecessary transshipment of goods.

We need not discuss MFN clauses further here, except to note that although the discrimination among foreign trading sources is widely recognized to be undesirable, the discrimination against all foreign traders, through tariff or quota restrictions, seems to be broadly accepted in public attitudes. It is as if the generalization principle has normative standing if applied within relevant classes or groups but it loses such standing as an argument that all producer groups, including those that sell goods to foreign markets or goods that are not import substitutes, should be treated symmetrically with those who seek to exclude foreign suppliers.

Given the failure of public attitudes to accept the appropriateness of extending the generality principle to foreign trade, it is surprising that politicized restrictions, even in these markets, remain relatively limited. International economic policy, and especially in the decades following World War II, seems to have been motivated by considerations that may reflect, at base, bad economic theory but that, at the same time, embodies an appreciation that excessively discriminatory political action must be held in check.

8 The political efficiency of general taxation[1]

This chapter concentrates on the politics of taxation. The interdependence between the workings of majoritarian democracy, as it is observed to operate in the United States in the 1990s, and the distribution of tax shares among persons and groups becomes our focal point of attention. The emergent results of this interdependence are, of course, affected by the constraints of the effective constitution – the rules of politics – as these are interpreted and enforced. And it is necessary to emphasize that the effective fiscal constitution, as it exists, does embody constraints that prevent many arbitrary departures from generality in tax treatment among persons and groups. It is widely acknowledged that the tax system, as observed in the United States near century's end, is less discriminatory than the expenditure system – the distribution of public spending benefits on the complementary side of the budget. That is to say, implementation of any generality norm may be closer to realization on the taxing side of the account. The question reduces to whether improvements can be made by moving toward further generality in treatment.

In a sense, our whole normative enterprise consists in constitutional evaluation, criticism, and suggestions for basic reforms. We ask, and try to answer, the question of whether changes in constitutional constraints on the taxing authority of governments, and notably those implied by moving toward implementation of the generality norm, can be expected to generate a more desirable pattern of outcomes. We suggest that movements toward generality in taxation will be "efficient," even if attainment of some ideal remains far from reach.

Proposals for changes in tax structure can be classified in two sets: those that increase discrimination or differentiation among persons and groups subject to tax (e.g., the Earned Income Tax Credit introduced in 1994) and those that reduce such discrimination and differentiation (e.g., the 1986 reduction in the number of rate brackets or, indeed, any of the flat-rate schemes discussed in 1995 and 1996). The central argument of this book offers what we think is clear-cut support for any and all reforms that may be classified to fall within the second of these two sets.

We shall first, in Section A, compare and contrast the principle of generality with other normative principles for the distribution of tax shares. Consideration of the alternative organizational principles reveals the political presuppositions upon which their advocacy depends. The difficulty of describing, precisely, the meaning of generality in taxation is discussed at some length, and especially as this description relates to several relevant issues of polity reform. What, precisely, does "equal treatment" mean with respect to the distribution of tax liabilities among persons? Equal-per-head levies? Flat-rate proportionality? Rate progressivity? Full income taxation? Imputed income inclusion? Exemption of saving? This preliminary and partial listing alone suggests that the whole index of traditional–conventional issues in normative tax theory can, if desired, be discussed in relation to the generality norm.

85

Generality is, of course, not the only principle that may be accepted as an objective in tax share distribution, even for majoritarian democracy. Trade-offs between changes that tend to satisfy the generality norm and other objectives may be necessary in any politically relevant discussion of fiscal reform. Fortunately, the organizational format of this book does not require us to enter into such comparative evaluation.

A. The efficiency of taxation under alternative political regimes

We have suggested that general taxation is more efficient than alternative tax-share schemes in a political regime broadly defined as a majoritarian democracy. It is first necessary to clarify the meaning of *efficiency* here because the claim made on behalf of general taxation may seem to run counter to much of the traditional tax analysis. Efficiency is used in its standard meaning – a tax structure is inefficient to the extent that it reduces aggregate economic value below that level which might be potentially achievable with a given resource, technological, and behavioral constraints, but under a modified set of constitutional rules. The critical interdependence stressed here is that between the overall efficiency of a tax-share system and the political structure within which taxing decisions are made. An institution that is classified to be relatively efficient in one constitutional order may be ranked quite differently in alternative political settings.

We need to specify more precisely the basic institutional framework summarized under the rubric majoritarian democracy. We assume the presence of a constitutional regime described by individual liberty, private ownership of property, and a market economy, which is subject, however, to politicization through the operation of majority decision rules in legislative assemblies – politicization that is relatively unconstrained regarding the range and scope of governmental action on either the spending or the taxing side of the fiscal account. The claim is that, in this political setting, a tax structure characterized by *generality* in the treatment of persons and/or other objects of imposition will involve a lower wastage of economic resources than alternative structures.

This claim differs from those commonly advanced in normative tax theory, primarily because the more familiar claims are made in total disregard of the political structure through which taxing decisions are made. Within such an arbitrarily imposed construction, the indirect feedbacks of tax structures on the efficiency of politics itself cannot be considered at all. To demonstrate the distinction between the efficiency of taxation defined in the conventional sense and the more inclusive concept of political efficiency, it will be helpful to discuss first two familiar conceptual frameworks for the development of normative propositions on tax-share distribution.

1. Minimization of utility loss under equirevenue assumptions

The first, and more traditional, model concentrates attention on the distribution of taxes in isolation from the spending or outlay side of the fiscal account. This whole exercise is based on some implicit assumption that the size and composition of the government's budget are beyond the competence of normative advice, and, further, that the distribution of taxes, as such, exerts little or no feedback effects, either positive or normative, on those forces that do, in fact, determine the allocation and size of governmental outlay. This approach became the starting point or base for the nineteenth-century utilitarian norm that dictated tax distribution in accordance with the principle of equimarginal sacrifice – a principle that generates "least aggregate sacrifice" in utility – as conceptually aggregated over the whole membership of the community. With plausibly acceptable notions about similarities among persons as utility generators, this principle of least aggregate sacrifice was used to justify differentiation in rates of tax by income or wealth criteria; that is, to justify or support progressive rate structures.

The normative argument for the differentiation in tax rates describing progressivity survived modern criticisms of utilitarianism as an internally coherent philosophical position with practicable implications. Even if it is acknowledged that individual utilities cannot be compared interpersonally and aggregated across persons, individualized utility losses that are generated by behavioral adjustments to taxes can be measured approximately. The "excess burden" of taxation, geometrically measured in the familiar welfare triangles, is a deadweight loss, no matter where the incidence finally rests. And the minimization of this loss appears to take on more concrete reality as an objective than the earlier targets that seemed more explicitly utilitarian. The modern normative theories of tax distribution emerged to justify differentiation in rates through highly sophisticated analytical models of social welfare maximization. Implicit in all of the exercises in "optimal taxation" are necessary presumptions about interpersonal comparisons of utilities. And, importantly, the same normative analysis is used to suggest that there are pure gains in economic efficiency, strictly interpreted, by differentiation in rates among nonpersonal bases for taxation (i.e., among goods and services) when these define criteria for tax liability.

Note that nowhere in the whole of this approach to taxation is there any recognition that persons and groups will invest valuable resources in the politics that may operate to produce favorable or unfavorable tax treatment.

2. Taxation in fiscal exchange[2]

As indicated earlier, there is an alternative approach or model that also falls within conventional normative analysis, although this second approach remains somewhat less familiar than the first. In this conceptualization of the taxing exercise, the distribution of tax shares among individuals and groups is not treated in isolation from the outlay side of the fiscal budget, and an explicit attempt is made to develop the bridge between taxing and spending. The central question posed is not simply about how tax shares should be allocated, given some exogenously determined revenue requirement, in order to achieve economic efficiency. Instead the question becomes the following: What is the efficient size of the budget, and how does the tax-share distribution interact to determine this size?

The answer emerges from a straightforward extension and application of the welfare criteria developed for the market or private sector of the economy. A necessary condition for efficiency in an economy that includes a public or collectivized sector is satisfied when the marginal costs of extending publicly financed goods or services are equated with the marginal values placed on such goods and services, summed over all persons in the sharing group. In its modern formulation, this solution was presented by Samuelson in his seminal 1954 paper (Samuelson, 1954). Earlier origins are found in works by Wicksell (1896) and Lindahl (1967, 1919). This approach offers normative justification for differentiated taxation in accordance with the separate demand intensities for publicly financed goods and services especially at the appropriately defined margins. The implied differentiation here may be broadly consistent with that which emerges from the utilitarian construction in some cases but may be quite inconsistent in others (Buchanan, 1964, 1976). The divergencies between the two approaches to tax-share distribution have prompted some modern tax analysts to suggest that the two principles be applied to separate sectors of the government budget (Musgrave, 1959).

Our purpose here is not to review in detail either of the two conventional models for tax norms. Instead, our purpose is to suggest that neither of the approaches sketched out previously embodies the necessary attention that must be paid to the politics through which any taxation must be processed and implemented. If government could indeed be modeled as a monolithic entity, the two approaches might be interpreted to yield diverse, but potentially useful, advice as to the allocation of tax shares among citizens in a polity. But if any such model of politics and governance is not descriptively accurate, even to some remote approximation, then the specific ordering of tax institutions that emerges from either of the two approaches may be misleading and, if introduced into political argument, may be counterproductive. That tax structure that is allegedly efficient if implemented through an idealized politics may be grossly inefficient when the feedback effects on the politics of its implementation are fully incorporated.[3]

3. Majority rule as a constitutional parameter

The point that we emphasize here was recognized by Wicksell, but it was not widely understood in the application that we develop because he sought to remedy the inconsistency between tax norms and democratic decision structures by modifying the latter rather than reexamining the former. That is to say, Wicksell proposed to change the rules that allow legislative majorities to make taxing-spending decisions for the community. He sought to ensure increased economic efficiency, appropriately defined, in the fiscal system by requiring more inclusive legislative agreement for collective action. In the idealized limit, Wicksell suggested the benchmark rule of unanimity. In practice, Wicksell suggested a qualified majority of some five-sixths of the members of the legislative body. With such a change in the decision rules, neither the distribution of tax shares nor of program benefits need be general or uniform. There is no direct argument for generality in treatment under the Wicksellian schemata.

An alternative means of moving toward some reconciliation of the potential inconsistency between political reality and tax norms, and the means that we discuss and analyze in this book, is to use the same starting point as Wicksell but to accept the institution of majority rule decision making as a constitutional parameter. Given the existence of this decision structure in politics, we then ask the same question posed earlier: What is the tax structure that seems most likely to yield the most efficient pattern of fiscal outcomes?

4. Constrained and unconstrained majority rule

There are two alternatives to be examined: Legislative majorities may be empowered to impose taxes without specific constraints or legislative majorities may be constrained constitutionally to the imposition of *general* taxation, with such a constraint applicable to the distribution of tax shares among persons and groups. The level of taxation may remain subject to majority determination.

We suggest that the second of these arrangements is constitutionally efficient in the sense that the generality requirement will produce patterns of fiscal outcomes that will minimize the destruction of economic value. In the perspective that recognizes the reality of politics, general taxation becomes first best constitutionally, even if it is acknowledged that qualifying tax-share distributions may remain second- or third-best from the idealized perspective of benevolent government.[4]

B. Majoritarian democracy

The reason that general taxation is more efficient than differential or discriminatory taxation in political democracy is that the very structure through which decisions are made prevents any attainment, even to some first approximation, of the type of tax-share discrimination that might be defined to be optimal in the stylized model that is altogether divorced from politics. That is to say, majoritarian processes cannot, by their nature, be expected to generate patterns of fiscal outcomes that embody the tax differentiation among persons and bases that correspond to that which might be yielded by some economist's detached apolitical advice – advice that translates into some implicit presumption that a benevolent despot holds effective fiscal authority.

As the more abstract models developed in earlier chapters have indicated, majority rule means what it says – rule by a majority coalition. This fact guarantees the emergence of discrimination in treatment between those who are members of the majority coalition and those who are not members, unless there exist constitutional constraints that prohibit or limit the exercise of such fiscal preference. Taxation is not different in this respect from any other activity of government.[5]

With generality in taxation in place as a constitutional constraint, majoritarian politics can work more or less as it is modeled to work in the standard textbook exercises of public-choice theory. In this setting, majority voting generates outcomes that reflect the preferences of the median voter for the overall level of taxation and, by inference, the size of the budget. When no such constraints exist, majority voting will ensure that one part of the inclusive constituency is maximally exploited through the fiscal process while members of the dominating majority coalition secure substantially all of the benefits from collective action.

The logic of the analysis here is straightforward, as has been demonstrated in the more abstract formulations in earlier chapters. It is perhaps surprising that public-choice theorists, in particular, have not concentrated more attention on majoritarian exploitation relative to their emphasis on median voter dominance. In part, this neglect may stem from a failure to recognize that fiscal politics is not really analogous to committee deliberation and that the alternatives for collective choice are endogenous to the process of selection itself rather than exogenously determined. Unless constrained otherwise, majorities must coalesce around alternatives that embody differential treatment among members of the inclusive political constituency.

Consider a highly simplified example, that of a three-person (or group) political community, the constitution for which dictates that collective actions are to be determined by a majority voting rule. Further, we restrict the alternatives to three discrete rates of tax that may be imposed on the income of each person, with levels of collective outlay being residually determined. We presume that this outlay is for the financing of genuinely collective consumption or public goods and that the distribution of benefits, as such, does not exert feedback effects on tax preferences.

We designate the three rates of tax as *high* (H), *medium* (M), and *low* (L). There are twenty-seven possible distributions of these three rates among the three persons, but only three of these distributions reflect symmetry or nondifferential treatment:

$$(HHH), \quad (MMM), \quad (LLL). \tag{1}$$

If fiscal choice should be restricted to these three options, majority voting would generate a solution that represents the preferred alternative of the median voter, provided that preferences could be arrayed to exhibit single peakedness.[6] And unless there are significant increasing returns to scale in budgetary size, single peakedness would seem characteristic of individual preferences. Presumably, for any given budgetary outlay, all persons prefer lower to higher rates of tax and, for any given rate of tax, higher to lower rates of outlay on the public good.[7]

Suppose that preferences are such that (MMM) would be the majority equilibrium if the options are constrained to satisfy the generality norm; that is, constrained to the three alternatives in (1). Under plausible assumptions about aggregate budget size and public goods evaluation in relation to the three rates of tax in the absence of a generality constraint, the imputation in (1), any one of the three, would be dominated *for some majority* by one or the other of the following sets of tax rates:

$$(LLH), \quad (LHL), \quad (HLL). \tag{2}$$

These imputations may be called, following von Neumann and Morgenstern (1944), the *solution set for the nonconstrained majoritarian game over tax rates*. A person would prefer that her own rate of tax be low while rates for others be high because of the presumed benefits of public outlay. Far from producing some middle or compromise outcome, majority voting must, in the nonconstrained case, guarantee maximal differentiation between members of majority and minority coalitions.

C. Efficiency implications

Important implications may be drawn from the comparison between the median preference outcome under the generality constraint and the set of majoritarian outcomes in (2), with no constraints. Given the constitutional generality requirement, so long as underlying preferences remain stable, the symmetrical solution (*MMM*) remains an equilibrium. Particular persons may, of course, prefer one of the other possible solutions, either (*HHH*) or (*LLL*), but if (*MMM*) is the majority equilibrium, under the generality constraint, the persons on either side of the median preference holder would find it relatively nonproductive to invest resources in efforts to secure an alternative outcome. An alternative outcome would be preferred by each one of the persons whose preferences were not met, but each would prefer a solution on a different side of the majority equilibrium. Differentially favored treatment is necessarily precluded by the generality constraint. Investment in political rent seeking is minimal relative to that which might take place in the absence of such constraint.

We can compare and contrast such relative quiescence with the situation confronted by a person in any of the imputations included in (2) – the set of nonconstrained majoritarian outcomes. The person who finds herself in the fiscally exploited minority position has a continuing incentive to convince one or the other of the other persons to leave the majority coalition and to join forces in the formation of a new majority. At the same time, each person in the majority will retain an incentive to convince her partner to remain in the coalition. There are strong incentives for each of the three persons to invest resources in political rent seeking, and such efforts may take several forms, including side agreements for adjustments in nontaxing dimensions of collective action. Prospects for majoritarian cycling among tax structures appear here in a near-classical sense. And, even if our simple models here seem far removed from political reality, they do suggest that we should not be at all surprised that legislative majorities are observed to be almost always engaged in alleged "tax reform."

The simplified model suggests that in the nonconstrained setting there will be continuous cycling along with instability in the distribution of tax shares. This implication is attenuated in effect when the model is adjusted to allow for different potential exploitability among the separate taxpayers–voters. If rates of tax are applied to an income base and if incomes are unequal pretax, then that majority coalition that maximally exploits the high-income recipient tends to be more stable than either of the alternatives in the inclusive majoritarian set. The reason is simple. Adjusted for relative group size, members of the exploiting majority have more to gain from tax discrimination against the rich than against the middle- or low-income groups. Cyclical prospects reemerge, however, when, as, and if rich persons recognize their fiscal vulnerability and invest in innovative cross-budgetary adjustments along with other politically effective "bribes."

A second related, but much more familiar, source of relative inefficiency in discriminatory as compared with general taxation is located in the necessary administrative costs that the former imposes both on government, as tax collector, and on the individual, as taxpayer. With differentials in rates of tax on different persons and/or different bases of tax, identification and classification become necessary. Complex enforcement schemes become essential if individual response patterns include efforts to reduce tax liabilities. Taxpayers, on the other hand, undergo costs in making these same efforts to limit liabilities for tax. The ancient precept for simplicity in taxation is increasingly violated as the structure moves away from generality.

Still another source of inefficiency generated by the workings of majoritarian politics is found in the differential excess burdens that arise from the predicted high-tax exploitation of political minorities. In the simplified three-person example, the majoritarian solution set includes only those imputations that involve maximal rates for one of the three persons, along with minimal rates for members of the minority. If either of the imputations in (2) is compared with the symmetrical imputation (*MMM*), which we assumed to reflect the median preference under the generality constraint, there is a higher excess burden in the former because of the asymmetry between loss and gain functions traced out by increases and decreases in rates (Brennan and Buchanan, 1981b, 1983). Strictly interpreted, this conclusion depends on the assumption that persons are identical in response behavior, but a less rigorous statement of the relationship noted would seem to hold even in the presence of substantial differences. General and uniform rates of tax tend to produce lower excess burdens than the differential taxation that would likely emerge from majoritarian democratic politics. This predictive statement in no way contradicts the traditional tax theorists' claim that there will always exist some ideally drawn schedule of discriminatory taxation that will absolutely minimize burdens.[8]

When a dynamic perspective is adopted, the inefficiency-generating properties of majority decision making take on greater significance. Members of any temporary majority coalition will have incentives to use the taxing power to exploit maximally members of the minority. But precisely because any majority coalition is impermanent, members will not act to maximize present values of revenues that might be extracted. Instead, rates of tax will be higher than those that would maximize present values. The short-run Laffer relationship dictates higher rates of tax than any long-run relationship (Buchanan and Lee, 1982). The nonconstrained fiscal operation of majoritarian democracy will almost surely produce lower rates of growth in the economy than would be the case under conditions when a constitutional requirement for generality in taxation is present.

To this point, we have identified and discussed several sources of economic inefficiency directly associated with an absence of a generality constraint on the taxing authority of government in majoritarian democracy: First, the incentives provided for wasteful rent seeking; second, the related costs of administration, both for government and taxpayers; and, third, the additional excess burdens involved when discrimination is introduced. A fourth possible source for inefficiency to be considered concerns the predicted effects of the nongenerality of taxes on the size and composition of the public or collective sector of the economy; that is, on the budget itself.

Early public-choice arguments suggested that majority voting rules generate budgets that are too large by ordinary efficiency criteria. These arguments were based on the presumption that taxes are levied generally, or at least that tax incidence is more general than benefit distribution (Buchanan and Tullock, 1962). If discrimination in both taxes and benefits (including transfers) is nonconstrained, the tendency toward excessively large budgets may be even more pronounced because members of majority coalitions would, in this setting, confront relatively lower tax costs for any public program than would be the case under general taxation.

D. The meaning of generality in taxation

We have discussed the potential efficiency-enhancing properties of generality in taxation without specific definition of what generality must mean in the context that is considered to be relevant. In one sense, the generality norm must be defined operationally. Because the ultimate purpose is to constrain majoritarian politics in order to prevent the natural tendency to use the taxing authority discriminatorily, generality is present to the extent that such use is discouraged.

It is much easier to define movements or changes in tax structures directionally, as toward or away from generality, than it is to define the endpoint on the generality spectrum. For example, any increase in the number of rate brackets, special exemptions, or exclusions shifts taxation away from generality. Tax reform proposals can be classified by the generality criterion even if disagreement remains on just what tax system would meet the criterion in some idealized sense.

In a limited construction, an argument might be advanced to the effect that only equal-per-head taxes would fully satisfy the generality requirement. Such a structure would put the collective or public goods sector on all fours with market exchange in which each person confronts the same set of prices for all partitionable goods and services. In the market, however, persons may adjust quantities demanded to these uniform prices in accordance with their preferences. Differing persons can purchase–use–consume differing quantities of goods and services, whether such preference differences stem from income–endowment sources or from intrinsic tastes–values. Politicization of the supply of a good or service breaks the quantity adjustment process that is offered by the market. All members of the collective group must, in the limiting model, have available equal quantities of those goods and services that are publicly provided. The logic of politicization dictates that interpersonal adjustments in "prices" (in this case, tax prices) confronted by persons become at least partial substitutes for marketlike adjustments in quantities finally used.

In this conceptualization, the levy of a uniform or flat rate of tax on the defined base retains almost all of the properties of generality, even if the principle, as applied, is quite different from that present in market interaction. In our treatment to this point, we have assumed that a standard or flat-rate tax on a designated source or base, itself tied to the individual who is personally liable, meets the generality criterion. Such a characterization is acceptable, provided that it is understood to require that the exemption or exclusion of any particular subsource or person becomes equivalent to the levy of zero rates and, hence, must violate any version of a generality norm. If, for example, personal income is to be the base upon which tax liabilities are imposed, generality requires imposition of the same rate on all sources of income, to all persons, with no exceptions and for any reason. The presence of any deduction, exclusion, or exemption must act to drive a political wedge between those who are subjected to positive rates, even if these rates are the same over all persons in the taxed group, and those who are differentially favored by zero rates. One of the disturbing features of several of the modern (1990s) proposals for tax reform has been the removal of persons from the income tax rolls – a change that exacerbates distributional conflict and one that clearly moves away from the generality norm.

A major issue in normative tax theory has been bypassed to this point by our assumption that income, if used as the basis for determining personal tax liability, can itself be readily defined in such a way as to command universal acceptance. This assumption is, of course, without foundation, and long-standing controversy over some of the definitional issues has characterized almost all arguments about tax changes. Specifically, for a starter, should "income as received" or "income as spent" become the basis for taxation, even if rates, once applied, are to be uniform over all persons? Advocates of spending-based taxation have long argued that savings must be excluded in order to avoid discriminatory double taxation of income flows. On the other hand, to the extent that persons secure utility from accumulation, any exclusion of savings sets up a differential rate structure, as defined operationally in terms of potential behavior. Strict adherence to the generality norm here would seem to deny legitimacy to the argument for exempting savings from tax. Or, to put the point in a somewhat different way, a uniform-rate tax that exempts savings is less general than a tax that does not contain any such exemption.

A closely related argument involves the treatment of capital gains. As the value of an asset increases, the net wealth of the owner increases. But is this increase (even if real in the sense that it is adjusted for inflation) to be counted properly as income for computing taxpayer liability?: As with the tax treatment of savings, the indicated implication of the generality norm suggests an affirmative response. Each of the sources of political inefficiency discussed earlier in this chapter comes into play if special treatment is accorded to capital gains. Clearly, the overall political efficiency of the tax structure is reduced if capital gains are taxed at favorable rates as compared with other sources.[9]

The principle of generality may, of course, be applied to other sources of taxation than personal incomes. Taxes may be imposed on the production, sale, or usage of goods and services. And such taxes can also be classified by the criterion of generality. The whole set of goods and services can be brought within the same tax structure under uniform rates. Or, differing rates (including zero) may be applied to different goods and services or to separate categories. As with the income tax base, the efficient set of rates that might be put in place by a benevolent fiscal authority would presumably embody some discrimination in rates and coverage. But in majoritarian politics, the dominant coalition of interests need not match the particular combination of interests that might produce optimal taxation. For more or less the same reasons as those discussed with reference to income taxation, there is an argument from political efficiency that supports general levies at uniform or across-the-board rates.

Both a flat-rate tax on all income or a uniform-rate tax on the sale–consumption or usage of all goods and services would meet most of the requirements for generality. If put in place institutionally, neither of these two structures would be grossly inefficient in the political sense stressed in this chapter. Rent-seeking efforts would be minimal. The choice between these two structures of general taxation would come down to some assessment of prospects for stability. Which of these two general tax systems would be least vulnerable to politically orchestrated manipulation? On this count, the flat rate of tax on income seems superior. A regime of general taxes applied to, say, sales of goods and services would be continuously vulnerable to coalitions of particular interests that might be formed in support of this or that category, with claims for deserved special treatment or exemption. The experience of the American state governments in this respect suggests that genuinely general, indirect taxation is not likely to be politically viable.

In summary, the tax system that most fully meets criteria for political efficiency would be the flat rate income tax, without exclusion or exemption. This system would correspond in many respects to the Hall–Rabushka (1983) proposal, which was introduced into the 1992 political debates by Jerry Brown, who seemed to understand fully the basic argument from political efficiency. A flat-rate tax scheme was introduced into the political debates in 1995 by Congressman Dick Armey and into the 1996 Republican primary elections by Steve Forbes. Most of these proposals were seriously flawed by failure to extend the flat rate of tax to all income earners, notably those at lower levels who were to be fully exempted from liability.

We should note that the flat-rate tax on income, considered independently of the uses of revenues, has no direct implications for the overall redistributive effects of the fiscal system. As such, the flat-rate tax is proportional to an income base. Whether the fiscal system, overall, is or is not redistributive and to what extent, depends on how program benefits, including transfers, are related to the pretax, prebenefit standings of persons. A flat tax on income combined with a budget that provides roughly equal-per-head benefits would, of course, be redistributive in impact, with some potential for continuing distributional argument in political discourse. But, as noted in the abstract examples in earlier chapters, the debates would be centered on alternatives that all lie "on the diagonal" as opposed to those that reflect nongeneral treatment in taxation and/or spending.

E. Conclusion

The efficiency-based argument for general taxation suggests only one avenue for reform in the operation of domestic politics in the United States at century's end. This politics has become increasingly distributional; members of Congress have come to be increasingly occupied in promoting particular interests, whether these be geographically or otherwise defined. The "politics of pork" tends to dominate considerations of general or all-encompassing interests. Traditionally, pork-barrel politics has been associated with the distribution of spending projects and the distribution of regulatory protections. Traditionally, the presumption has been that there remains sufficient generality in taxation to warrant relatively less concern about the issues examined in this chapter.

The distribution of tax shares among citizens does, in fact, meet any generality criterion more fully than the distribution of fiscal benefits and transfers on the other side of the budget account. The basis for the discrepancy here lies in legal–political history. Constitutional limits on discrimination in taxation have been interpreted to be more constraining than comparable limits on spending (Tuerck, 1967). The rule of law has been applied in such a fashion as to prevent arbitrary discrimination in the assignment of tax liabilities. Persons cannot be subjected to differentially burdensome taxes merely because they hold membership in minority political coalitions or parties, as the abstract models of majoritarian politics might imply. Discrimination in tax shares must be based on criteria that seem, nominally, to be, themselves, general in nature. As interpreted, the Constitution prevents persons from being subjected to differentially unfavorable taxation on the basis of noneconomic characteristics such as gender, race, ethnicity, religion, height, weight, or physical appearance. Legislative majorities cannot discriminate to the detail that members might prefer. But tax rates can be varied over a wide set of economic characteristics: income and wealth classes, occupations, professions, and industrial categories. Race horse breeders, real estate developers, and resort operators can secure special treatment without constitutional challenge.

The rule of law, as interpreted with reference to the allocation of tax shares, stands as a remaining constitutional constraint against the natural proclivity of majoritarian politics. Any movement away from uniformity can only exacerbate political conflict and reduce the efficiency of the fiscal system.[10]

9 Deficit financing and intertemporal discrimination

As we have previously noted, the analytical structure of this book is simple and involves a single theme. We have repeatedly used the two-person matrix metaphor to demonstrate that, by its own logic, majoritarian politics must violate the generality precept. Outcomes tend to be off the diagonal, and only the potential rotation of majority coalitions indirectly legitimizes the whole process. The economic argument for imposing a generality constraint constitutionally is based on predictions about the relative inefficiency of off-diagonal outcomes, as measured both in the orthodox allocative sense of neoclassical economics and in the public-choice, rent-seeking sense of minimizing resource wastage.

We have discussed only briefly (Chapter 6) temporal characteristics of the political setting, despite the obvious fact that, even as stylized, majoritarian rotation requires a time sequence. Implicitly, it is as if we assume an inclusive constituency of long-lived participants, whose effective planning horizons are sufficiently extended to allow for nonbiased expectations concerning membership in successful and unsuccessful political coalitions.

The two-person (or coalition) matrix metaphor is useful in this postulated setting. To the extent that rotation among the off-diagonal positions generates a pattern of outcomes that is deemed to be relatively inefficient, *all* parties to the collective interaction may be persuaded to agree on a constitutional constraint that requires generality – a constraint that dictates in-period equality in political treatment, at least as an idealized objective. The separate applications discussed in the immediately preceding and following chapters can all be brought within this analytical umbrella.

This chapter departs from the common analytical structure, and the argument is necessarily more complex. Here we discuss a departure from the generality norm that cannot be analyzed satisfactorily with the atemporal metaphor. Here it becomes necessary specifically to include reference to the time dimension of politics – to the temporal elements of political action. The financing of governmental outlay by borrowing rather than taxation is the object of attention. And, interestingly, although the electoral competition that describes majoritarian politics is a major causal factor in deficit creation, the particular authority granted to majority coalitions, vis-à-vis members of excluded minority members, is not of central importance. Those who are exploited by deficit financing are not persons who are currently excluded from the majority coalition that exercises decision-making power, as is the case in the other applications discussed. Instead, those who are exploited fiscally by deficit financing are all members of the polity who might face tax liabilities in periods subsequent to that in which the financing–spending decision is made. For shorthand reference, "future generations" are exploited by the "present generation."

It is first necessary to demonstrate that deficit financing does, indeed, represent a departure from the generality norm. Section A covers this material that is extended in Section B to include the Ricardian proposition on neutrality. In Section C, the discussion concentrates on the relationship between capital budgeting, debt financing, and generality. In Section D, we discuss the proposed constitutional requirement for budget balance in the context of the generality principle. Section E examines intergenerational generality with respect to problems that might arise in efforts to retire outstanding public debt. Section F concludes the chapter.

A. Deficit financing and intertemporal generality

Consider, first, a stylized setting in which a genuinely public good yields current-period benefits that are made generally available to all members of the inclusive political community and is financed by a general flat-rate or proportional tax on all units of income as currently received. That is to say, the generality norm is satisfied to the maximal extent. The quantity of the public good, and hence the size of the budget, as well as the rate of the tax, is determined by majority voting. If persons are assumed to exhibit standard nonconvexities in utility functions, the solution will reflect the preferences of the median voter, among the choice alternatives, all of which lie along the diagonal. Preferences for the amount or quantity of public goods will differ among persons because of differing evaluations of the good relative to others, which may, in turn, reflect differing personal positions along an income–wealth scalar as well as differing tastes. But there is no overt fiscal exploitation in the sense that a majority coalition uses its authority either to extract differential payment from members of the minority or to secure differential partitionable benefits for its own members.

Now consider a change in fiscal regime. Assume, as before, that the good to be financed meets publicness criteria and is made generally available to all members of the inclusive constituency. But now assume that rather than being financed by the general flat-rate tax on all units of income, as received by separate persons, the outlay is financed by the issue of government debt. Persons are not subjected to tax; government sells debt instruments (bonds) to whomever wants, voluntarily, to purchase them, whether citizens or foreigners. Purchasers transfer current purchasing power to government in exchange for the promised interest payments on the securities, along with a guarantee of redemption of capital value or principal at some specified date. (For elementary analysis see Buchanan, 1958.)

Under this regime, all persons who are members of the polity, whether or not they may exhibit preferences at or near the median for the whole group, enjoy the benefits of the public good, but they do not have to sacrifice private value through coercive taxation. Clearly, these persons are differentially benefited by the exercise of political authority – benefited at the expense of persons who must be placed in the opposing position, in which they are politically coerced into making tax payments without receiving benefits in return. The relevant distinction between the two groups, whom we may designate as the *net beneficiaries* and the *net taxpayers*, respectively, is exclusively temporal. The members of the political constituency during the time period when the debt-financed benefits are actually consumed, used up, or enjoyed are differentially exploiting members of the political constituency during the time period when the taxes to service and amortize the debt must be paid. This fiscal regime violates the generality principle: persons are not subjected to equal treatment; there is an intertemporal departure, even if all of the other conditions required for a regime to qualify are satisfied.

B. Generality and the Ricardo–Barro theorem on debt neutrality

Robert Barro (1974) introduced modern economists to a theorem presented early in the nineteenth century by David Ricardo (1933/1817; Sraffa, ed., 1951) that was discussed in classical public finance (Buchanan, 1958). The theorem states that if constituents are fully rational, they will recognize the logical equivalence between financing governmental outlay by taxation and by borrowing. By definition, the present value of the stream of interest/amortization payments will be equal to the value of current-period taxes required to finance the same outlay. In their effects on personal behavior, the theorem states that the two financing instruments should be equivalent.

It is widely acknowledged that the conditions required to validate the Ricardo theorem are extremely restrictive. But these conditions are not central to our concern at this point. The question that we address is quite specific: Even under the conditions required to render the neutrality theorem applicable, would debt financing of outlay violate the intertemporal generality norm?

The answer is clearly in the affirmative. Whether current-period members of the political unit know that debt financing of currently consumed benefits generates future-period tax liabilities of equal present value is not germane to the temporal translation of costs from current to future periods. Indeed, the whole purpose of debt financing is to effect such a temporal transposition. This statement is equally applicable to the private behavior of a person, who may contract private debt, and to the behavior of an agent or agency charged with making decisions for the collectivity, whether this be a designated person, a majority coalition, or the inclusive constituency.

In the terminology that we have used previously, it is clear that any debt financing of currently enjoyed services involves explicit exploitation of future-period persons. The individual who takes out a pure consumption private loan that she knows must be repaid next week or next month is deliberately imposing an uncompensated burden on her future self in a temporal exchange for present-period benefits. Such a pattern of behavior can be described as intertemporal discrimination among the separate persons who make up the continuing unit of consciousness.

The extension to the collectivity is straightforward. Even under a rule of unanimity that, in itself, would ensure against majoritarian exploitation of a minority, and even if all persons have full knowledge of the present value of future taxes, a collective decision to borrow for current-period services amounts to differential or discriminatory treatment of potential taxpayers in future periods. It is as if all persons in Period One constitute a majority coalition that proceeds to exploit all persons who will be around to service the debt in Period Two and beyond.

This argument may be accepted, but proponents of the Ricardo theorem's validity may question the relevance of the result for any normative condemnation of such violation of generality. If persons know that any issue of public debt creates an equal present-value liability, and if they adjust their portfolios to maintain preferred generational allocational patterns, those Period Two (and beyond) persons will not be exploited overtly by a Period One decision to issue public debt. In this stylized Ricardo–Barro scenario, constituent taxpayers–borrowers in Period One fully absorb the burden of payment for currently enjoyed program benefits. There is, then, no transposition of value through time involved at all. Public debt issue is simply a means of taxation. There is no intertemporal discrimination, and hence no violation of the generality norm.

Something seems wrong with this line of argument. And it is relatively easy to discover the basic error once a public-choice perspective is adopted. If Ricardo–Barro behavior fully describes the reaction of persons to alternative financing instruments, there is, in effect, no collective analogue to private debt available. Persons, in their capacities as members of a body politic, are forestalled, by their own reactive behavior, from doing what they clearly seem able to do in private capacities. Think of a private equivalent to Ricardo–Barro adjustment; a person who adjusts fully her portfolio to offset the impact of an incurred debt obligation on capital values does not, in effect, borrow at all. The very meaning of borrowing is eliminated.

The *raison d'être* of borrowing, whether by a person in a private capacity, or by persons in a collective organization, in some government-as-agency capacity, is to implement the temporal transposition of value – to postpone until later periods the burden of payment for current outlay. In effect, the Ricardo–Barro proposition suggests that governments cannot borrow at all – a proposition that seems absurd on its face, quite apart from the overwhelming empirical evidence that political agents prefer to finance outlay by a mix of debt and taxes, rather than by taxes alone.

C. Public debt, public capital, and the generality principle

In describing the stylized model examined in preceding sections, we were careful to specify that the debt-financed program benefits were enjoyed or consumed during the period when the debt was issued and not during subsequent fiscal periods. In other words, we specified that the subject for analysis was the collective equivalent to a private consumption loan. In such a setting, it is almost self-evident that debt issue does indeed involve intertemporal discrimination that violates the generality norm.

If we modify this critical assumption about the temporal location of benefit flows, the use of public-debt financing, as such, does not necessarily imply intertemporal discrimination. There is a classical public finance normative argument in support of debt financing for public capital investment projects that are expected to yield benefits over a sequence of time periods subsequent to that in which the funds are borrowed and expended in the construction of the projects. Tax financing of such projects would violate the generality norm by imposing differential burdens reflected in current-period liabilities.

Uniform or equal treatment would require that temporal patterns of benefit flows and tax payments reflect some rough balance. Genuine borrowing to finance public projects that yields benefits over extended time sequences does not violate the generality precept. In a practical sense, some institutional separation between a capital and a current fiscal budget might be suggested, despite the sometimes difficult task of drawing the line between the two. Alternatively, the specific earmarking of future-period tax sources to service and amortize specific project-related issues of public debt might accomplish many of the same purposes.

Our purpose here is not to discuss particular features of capital budgeting. This section is introduced only to qualify the more general argument about the intertemporal discrimination that government borrowing represents.

D. Deficit financing and the generality norm in constitutional perspective

The argument suggests that the democratic process needs to be constrained along the debt–tax dimension if the generality principle is to be satisfied. That is to say, some version of a balanced budget constitutional requirement, appropriately adjusted to allow for special treatment for public investment projects, becomes a necessary part of the inclusive set of constitutional reforms that adherence to the generality precept would dictate.

As briefly noted earlier, however, there is a basic difference between the balanced budget constraint and those that might be designed for other applications, to welfare programs, to regulatory policy, and to taxation. In each of these applications, the interplay between majority rule politics and the benefits and costs of potential collective action can be modeled as a straightforward two-party game. In the classical setting, the rational basis for agreement on a binding constitutional constraint is evident. Each of the parties recognizes that opportunistic or in-period behavior will generate the off-diagonal sequence of results. Over the whole succession of periods, the rotational exploitation of one party by the other is less desirable than a rule-defined guarantee that the result, in each period, remains on the diagonal, that each party be subjected to equal treatment, in each period. Generality emerges as a feature of rationally based agreement by interacting persons.

No comparable derivation is possible in the setting in which the potentially exploited person or group is not, and cannot be, party to an agreement. By the nature of time itself, persons in future periods cannot be present now or, in the situation discussed here, cannot be present during the fiscal period when current outlay is financed by borrowing. At best, therefore, the origins of a rule that restricts resorting to public borrowing must be found in the calculus of present-period voters–agents. The inquiry suggests focus on the analysis of rules that have *self-control* as their purpose. In their private capacities, persons may impose constraints on their future-period behavior aimed to prevent predicted response to temptation – response that is considered undesirable from some long-term perspective. Ulysses offers the example from classical mythology (Elster, 1979). The logic is readily extended to persons in their public or collective capacities. A person, as voter or as political agent, may predict that, in future periods, the political attractiveness of financing outlay by debt rather than taxation will prove irresistible. Support for some constraint may be enhanced by a recognition that political agents respond to a multiplicity of voters and groups of interests. The individual may be less concerned with imposing constraints on her own future behavior than with imposing constraints on the behavior of some irresponsible others.

Note, however, that the constitutional calculus remains quite different in this setting than in those previously discussed. In the other settings, the individual may choose to impose a generality requirement because she fears potential exploitation by others in positions of collective authority. In the debt financing setting, the individual may not act from any fear that she, personally and currently, will be exploited fiscally in the absence of constraint. The fear that prompts the constraint against debt financing may be against future fiscal exploitation by political authority that is currently exercised. Hence, a person comes to support a balanced budget constraint only in some "representative" capacity, only as an agent for a future self or selves.

This book is not the place for detailed analysis of the difficulties that may be encountered in securing the implementation of a constraint for budget balance (Buchanan, Rowley, and Tollison, 1987). The objective for this chapter is limited to support for the proposition that continued budget imbalance involves a blatant disregard for the generality precept and that the discrimination involved is intergenerational rather than intercoalitional.

E. Debt retirement and the generality norm

Failure to finance public outlay through taxation ensures continued increase in the value of outstanding government debt, with the consequent increase in interest payments, which can only measure deadweight burden on the productive capacity of the national economy. Even if a constitutional requirement for budget balance should be put in place and fully honored, the debt that had been accumulated prior to the period when budget balance becomes reality (2002?) would require servicing.

Any proposal to pay off or retire any share of outstanding debt would necessarily include the use of currently collected revenues in excess of current-period outlay on public goods and transfers. Those persons subjected to the tax increment measured by the budget surplus could, quite legitimately, claim that they are fiscally exploited; they are subjected to discriminatory treatment by comparison with persons who live either in earlier or later fiscal periods. Why should any particular generation of taxpayers be singled out for differentially high taxation, without corresponding benefits, in order to reduce the tax obligations of all persons who will make up the membership of future generations? The generality principle emerges here as a relatively powerful argument against any policy of debt retirement. The "sins of the past," visited on all citizens of the polity by the initial incurrence of debt used to finance ordinary public consumption, should be borne equally across all generations. Or at least this would be the implication of the generality norm. To impose differential taxation on any time cohort of taxpayers merely to pay off debt is the fiscal equivalent to deficit financing in reverse. The latter discriminates in favor of the current citizenry; the former against the current citizenry.

Debt retirement is equivalent to the formation of capital. How is this statement related to the earlier discussion about debt financing of public investment projects? We suggested that strict adherence to the generality norm requires that public investments that yield streams of expected returns over a finite sequence of periods should be financed by debt instruments that correspond in maturities to projected benefit flows.

If, then, debt retirement is the same as the creation of public capital, why not finance such retirement by debt issue? The contradiction is apparent. Clearly, debt retirement must embody an explicitly chosen departure from the generality norm, again a departure that is precisely the opposite of that involved in deficit creation. Retirement of long-term debt reflects a decision by current-period political agents to discriminate against current-period taxpayers for the benefit of persons who will be members of the political community in the future. The private analogue to public debt retirement is the creation of capital from income that would otherwise be available for current consumption purposes.

There are, of course, several public-choice bases for predicting that explicit policies for debt retirement will be difficult to introduce. These analytics need not be discussed here. It is sufficient to indicate only that, to the extent that the generality principle does inform political discourse and despite the absence of formal constraints, the discriminatory treatment that debt retirement must represent enters the argument with significant negative weight.

F. Conclusions

The analysis in this chapter differs from the others that examine other applications of the generality principle or the departures therefrom. In other applications, the generality constraint, if introduced and enforced as a restriction on the interest-motivated choices of majority coalitions, acts to prevent, or at least to limit, overt fiscal exploitation of one group by another, when all members of both groups are temporally equivalent; all persons are present in the here and now. That is to say, the political discrimination that is constrained is not temporal.

In this respect, the departure from generality that debt-financed public consumption represents is categorically different. The political discrimination is exclusively temporal, and a constraint acts to prevent or limit the exploitation of future-period persons by those who are beneficiaries of current public programs. The decision rule, whether effective fiscal choices are made by a majority coalition, a ruling minority, or even by consensus among all citizens, does not enter so directly into the calculus. Any decision rule must exclude from the effective coalition those persons who will only be present in future periods, when the fiscal burdens of debt must be experienced.

In a sense, a generality constraint is needed here even more because of the absence of any temporal analogue to the rotation of majority coalitions. There is simply no means through which future-period taxpayers, who are exploited by debt financing, can "get back" at current-period exploiters.

10 Generality and the supply of public services

In Chapter 8, we suggested that *general* taxation is an efficient revenue-raising institution in majoritarian democracy. We did not explicitly relate the analysis to the outlay or spending side of the fiscal account. Implicitly, however, the presumption was that revenues raised by taxes are devoted to the financing of public or collective consumption goods and services, which, as provided, are available to all members of the political community. That is to say, the analysis of tax alternatives proceeded on the presumption that spending benefits are, themselves, *general* in this publicness or availability sense. Individual evaluations of publicly financed goods and services may, of course, differ widely, but the stylized model, as examined, involved no explicit politically determined differentiation among beneficiaries. As in the simple exercises of earlier chapters, the classic example is David Hume's meadow that needs to be drained to the prospective benefit of all adjacent farmers. The subject matter to be examined in this chapter includes other types of government services as well. We propose to analyze the workings of majoritarian politics in a constitutional setting that allows government spending that is not limited to the financing of technologically defined public goods but is directed also to the financing and production of goods and services that may be partitioned among separate users. We hold off analysis of direct monetary transfers until Chapter 11.

There are many distinctions between an individual's effective demand for services acquired via market exchange transactions and goods and services that may be acquired through governmental–political auspices. A distinction that is relevant for the present analysis is that the effective personal demand for private goods is determined by the willingness of individuals to purchase output made available by profit-seeking firms at various prices, whereas the effective demand for government services emerges in the willingness of (some) individuals to take steps to influence the organization of government supply of particular services *before* production, itself, takes place. An individual's inclination to participate in the political process that ultimately determines output levels is in part dependent on the expected distribution of benefits and costs associated with those outputs. How much does an individual stand to gain or lose from alternative policies that might be adopted? How the services themselves are distributed, whether profits or rents accrue to factors engaged in the production of those services, and the rate at which personal tax burden increases with increases in quantity of services provided – all of these variables affect an individual's demand for governmental action.

Political institutions determine what an individual must sacrifice in order to exert influence on the final production of government services. By classifying legitimate channels of influence and defining the penalties associated with illegal efforts, political institutions determine the effectiveness of alternative methods of participating in the collective decision-making process. For example, initiating support for a policy alternative, organizing political parties, and, finally, casting a vote are more effective in a democracy than in a dictatorship. Many one-party states go through the motions of an electoral process, but most persons do not consider their votes as affecting political outcomes. And, even in genuinely democratic regimes, voting, as such, is more effective in a direct referendum than in any indirect selection of a legislator. Similarly, lobbying for specific government services or particular methods of production is more easily undertaken if such activities are legal. Any such pressure-group effort is more effective when policymakers (legislators) have discretion to select policy alternatives, than when they do not. And, such efforts are more effective if policymakers have incentives to take account of those actively attempting to influence the policies chosen. The effectiveness of lobbying is, thus, affected by formal institutions that constrain, punish, and reward policymakers for their decisions and by informal cultural constraints that identify legitimate and illegitimate opportunism by government agents.

In the production and distribution of government services, modern formal institutions provide numerous opportunities for consumers and producers of these services to lobby for preferential treatment. These opportunities again suggest that adherence to a generality principle as an institution may increase political efficiency. In this chapter we demonstrate that constraining democratic governments to distribute, produce, and finance goods and services supplied in accordance with the generality principle increases the efficiency of collective decision making.

A. Generality and the distribution of government services

The classic economic case for government intervention is offered by the presumed existence of pure public goods. A pure public good exhibits nonrivalry in consumption and is often produced in a manner that precludes exclusion (Samuelson, 1954). The standard argument is direct: Private (market) production of genuinely public goods tends to be suboptimal because self-interested individuals only take account of their own share of the benefits when producing or purchasing such goods and services. That is to say, from the vantage point of a single individual, all goods are "private." Neglect of the spillover benefits at the margin implies that unrealized gains from trade exist among all those who consume the good in question. In a fully voluntaristic equilibrium under market provision, relatively low demanders of the common consumption goods free ride on the efforts of high demanders, although even such low demanders would be willing to contribute at the margin to secure increased levels of provision. Collective (government) provision can correct for the shortfall by using state coercion (taxation) to fund a level of the public good or service that would satisfy the Pareto or Wicksellian norm for efficiency. Moreover, in principle, taxes can be apportioned so that everyone in the polity can secure positive net benefits from extension of production. The realization of such potential gains from the financing and production of pure public goods and services plays a central role in the contractarian rationale for the formation and operation of what has been called the *productive state*.

Of course, governments produce many other kinds of goods and services in addition to those technically classified as public goods. For example, there is a class of goods that exhibits some rivalry in consumption but that has production technologies that make exclusion impractical and private provision thereby unprofitable. National defense is generally a government service that is uniformly provided to all within a country, in the sense that all those within the borders of the country receive essentially the same protection. The technology of defense makes it impractical to provide "national defense"on a citizen-by-citizen or household-by-household basis because potential invasions are more easily repelled along a single external border than along the many, and longer, disjoined borders that would result from a mosaic of defended households. Other common government services exhibit similar geographical economies, albeit on a smaller scale. House-by-house fire or police protection does little good (or is very expensive) in densely populated areas because unprotected houses pose a threat to neighbors. Such services often cost little more to provide to a whole neighborhood or region than to a single dwelling in the neighborhood. (Some may cost less.)

Again, the case for public provision seems straightforward. Were such services provided privately via voluntary subscription, those who believe they receive no benefits would be relieved from sharing the cost of an undesired "service," but many others who do value the services would be able to free ride on those who actually subscribe. The free riders both *reduce* the value of the service received by subscribers and *increase* the cost of extension. Service levels under private subscription would be too small, in efficiency terms, and, in the extreme case, there may be no supply at all. Everyone in the relevant service area could potentially benefit from higher levels of provision under appropriate cost-sharing arrangements. Extreme economies of scale in the provision of services, together with free-riding problems associated with imperfect exclusion, often require some coordinated collective effort to secure the service in question.[1] As a remedy to the problem of joint supply, individuals receive such services whether they value them or not.

Many other government services are produced in which exclusion is readily accomplished and the normative case for government provision is less clear-cut. Government services such as highways, higher education, parks, medical care, and legal advice principally benefit the recipients and have very little publicness. The ongoing debate as to whether such services are appropriate for government provision is beyond the scope of the current discussion here.

What is focused on here is whether all government services should be uniformly available to all voters within the polity of interest regardless of whether exclusion is technologically feasible. The uniform provision of nonexcludable services is a consequence of fundamental technological characteristics. Only general policies about the level of production are possible for such goods. By contrast, the uniform, or general, provision of potentially excludable services is a consequence of political rather than technological processes. Generality is an explicit policy constraint only for such potentially excludable government services. As before, we conduct our analysis of the political merits of the generality rule as applied to the distribution of government goods and/or services in a two-player, two-matrix interaction in order to simplify exposition.

Consider the two-by-two matrix in Figure 10.1 describing the benefits, net of tax, received from government service by each of two individuals (or coalitions) in the

B

		Receives the Service Generally	Receives the Service Differentially
A	Receives the Service Generally	I 1, 1	II -1, 2
	Receives the Service Differentially	III 2, -1	IV 0, 0

Figure 10.1. The discrimination dilemma.

polity of interest.[2] The off-diagonal cells represent unequal consumption levels of the publicly supplied service financed with revenues from general taxation. Were the service in question a nonexcludable pure public good, only uniform availability would be possible, and solutions would be restricted to the diagonal. In this case, both *A* and *B* would prefer Cell I to Cell IV.

This result no longer holds if the government service in question is potentially excludable. In this case, if either *B* or *A* has the power to determine the distribution, each would opt for a directed and discriminatory distribution. *B* prefers Cell II, and *A* prefers Cell III. The opportunity to use general revenues to advance private interests greatly reduces the decision maker's cost of securing desired goods and services. In the two-person example, the person in authority receives the full benefit but pays only half of the cost (under general taxation).

If neither party has the power to make policy directly, each may attempt to influence the decision of the party that does have decision authority. In the case in which the status quo is no collective action (Cell IV), each person would make some effort toward securing the good for herself alone, and this effort would be greater than that which would be made to secure joint provision. Under the assumption that the good or service is fully partitionable, only one-half the quantity could be consumed at the same per person tax cost. Under joint (equal) provision as under discriminatory provision, if the numerical payoffs in Figure 10.1 are treated as values, note that each person would expend up to two dollars (over taxes) to have the benefits exclusively but only one dollar to share benefits equally. On the other hand, incentives to lobby for narrow public services are weaker in the case in which services are provided uniformly than in the case in which the services are not provided at all. *A* and *B* are both prepared to pay up to one dollar to avoid funding the other party's share of the service in the case in which the status quo entails the uniform provision of the good.

Of course, preferring special treatment is one thing and securing it is another. The victim of any narrow provision of this public service is prepared to spend up to two dollars to move from discriminatory provision of the government service to uniform provision. The beneficiary of discriminatory provision is only willing to pay one dollar to assure his privileged status. Consequently, in cases where returns to lobbying are equal, each coalition would be equally likely to emerge and where voting determines policy. Distributional aspects of public service provision allow the possibility of majority cycles. *A* and *B* each may secure special privileges in the short run but be bound to lose them in the long run as the vagaries of voter turnout, coalition stability problems, and ideological innovation eventually cause electoral winners to become electoral losers. In the numerical example, average benefits within an evenly rotating majoritarian cycle between *A* and *B* are fifty cents.

Adherence to a generality principle reduces the range of fiscal policies that may be chosen in a manner that tends to increase average net benefits for all parties. A generality constraint on the distribution of government services eliminates the possibility of preferential treatment and constrains any conflict that might remain on the fiscal diagonal (regarding appropriate equal-service levels). Generality thereby eliminates, or at least greatly reduces, incentives to invest resources in coalitional conflict. In the symmetric two-output case described, service-level conflict is replaced by complete consensus. The generality principle, similarly, reduces the scope for majoritarian cycles to those that might lie upon the fiscal diagonal. In the example, escape from the evenly rotating off-diagonal majority cycle between *A* and *B* yields a stable service level that increases each party's average net payoff from fifty cents to one dollar.

The argument for providing potentially excludable government services *as if* they were nonexcludable public goods has largely paralleled our previous analysis. Any departure from generality in the distribution of public services necessarily creates incentives for the formation of majority coalitions in support of differentially advantageous distribution of publicly financed services. Potential departures from generality ensure that majority cycles are likely to occur.

All government services are effectively public goods under a generality rule.[3] However, publicness, by itself, does not fully resolve the political decision-making problem of interest here. The politics of producing and financing a service that is distributed in a manner consistent with generality remains problematic.

B. Distributional aspects of the production of public services

Other than arguing that government goods and services should be purchased or produced at least cost, economists have contributed relatively little to the analysis of the manner in which such goods and services should be produced. Normative analysis, by and large, has focused on optimal levels of provision rather than on the properties of alternative methods for delivering the same service. Public-choice models have largely focused on the demands of voters, interest groups, and government agents. In cases where the government is simply another consumer in a larger competitive market, as when it purchases coffee, paper goods, or personal computers for small numbers of office workers, analysis of how and where a government purchases inputs may be a relatively uninteresting exercise. This situation may be faced by local governments and small national governments that purchase goods in extensive national or world markets. However, in cases in which government demand has significant effects upon the scale or concentration of particular markets, and thereby on the distribution of wealth, this neglect is less tenable. In such cases, the interest of suppliers in securing increased demands for their services may play a significant role in determining government output levels and/or the mix of services permitted.

These last cases are commonplace. Most government output decisions have significant effects on the distribution of personal wealth in at least some markets. Even in cases in which government purchases take place in large well-developed competitive markets, purchases are often on such a scale as to affect relative prices and thereby the profits and wages of those producing the goods. A good deal of United States agricultural policy in the past half century has been predicated on such effects. Similar effects are evident in cases in which government services are produced by industries that are concentrated in particular locations of the polity of interest.

In less extensive or less well-developed markets, efforts to promote competition at one stage of contracting often reduce competition at others. For example, a properly constructed contest among firms to secure exclusive rights to produce a particular government service clearly induces competition among potential suppliers, which allows the cost of government services to fall in the short run. The winner secures a monopoly position with respect to government, which directly affects market concentration insofar as the firm expands significantly to accommodate government demand. Exclusive contracts also indirectly affect concentration in the long run by affecting the distribution of talent, capital, experience, and profits among firms within the industry.

Some of these wealth effects are consequences of well-intentioned efforts to produce government services at least cost. The production of government services is often less costly when concentrated at a few discrete sites rather than distributed more uniformly across a whole territory. Realizing what might be called *locational economies of scale in production* increases the demand for locally immobile factors of production in a manner that affects the profits and quasi-rents acquired by essentially *all* immobile factors of production in the region of interest – whether directly involved in the production of government services or not. For example, large projects will affect both local real estate values and local wage rates (occasionally in opposite directions).[4]

There are direct beneficiaries of local government production and indirect losers. Demand for some immobile factors may fall as a consequence of the siting of noxious service facilities. The prices of residential property around an expanding landfill, prison, or airport often decline in the short run. In other cases, higher demand for immobile factors may increase the wealth of direct producers of government services but reduce that of owners of other firms who use those now more costly factors to produce products for export.

The wealth effects of the production of government services create incentives for firms and individuals to invest significant resources in lobbying government decision makers for contracts and for high levels of provisions regardless of whether demand for particular immobile factors rises or falls. Those who expect to gain from relative price changes induced by government contracts will lobby for increased quantities. Those who stand to lose from higher input prices will oppose local production contracts and favor lower service levels. To the extent that proservice lobbies are more effective than their counterparts, service levels will exceed those that would have been sufficient to satisfy consumer demands for government services (at given tax prices). Successive governing coalitions might shift production sites among regions and industries.

Consideration advanced here suggests that even if governmental activities meet criteria for generality on the demand side of the fiscal ledger, effective discrimination may describe the supply side. For example, a good or service may be both nonrivalrous and nonexcludable, hence genuinely "public" in the technological sense, but its production–supply may exhibit such "locational lumpiness" as to create the potential for differential rents or quasi-rents. The nuclear deterrence provided by the submarine produced in Connecticut is available for all citizens in the United States, but Connecticut residents exert differential effort to ensure submarine production.

C. Generality and efficiency in the production of public services

Application of the generality principle to the production of public goods and services requires that production decisions, themselves, should not confer benefits or costs on specific individuals, industries, or regions of the country. That is to say, the production, itself, of government services should not materially alter the distribution of wealth. Thus complete generality requires the *absence of significant relative price effects* in the production of government services. Even in cases in which a program is explicitly redistributional, as might be said of welfare and social security, generality requires that the relative prices of factors used to produce those services not be materially altered. Relative price neutrality implies that no firms or factors of production stand to profit or lose from decisions regarding the allocation of production among firms or regions. In this case, neither firms nor factory owners would have a particular interest in the level of government services provided. The pursuit of government contracts would attract neither more nor less interest than other business arrangements.

It bears noting that relative price neutrality and generality are identical only if neutrality holds at the *service-by-service* level of analysis. Aggregate price neutrality is not sufficient to reduce cycling and rent-seeking problems. Program A may drive up the demand for labor, whereas Program B may drive up the demand for capital. In this case, labor clearly would lobby for increases in Program A, whereas capital owners would lobby for increases in Program B. Majoritarian cycles between and among all such groups would generate significant changes in the composition of government output and the distribution of wealth. Neutrality in the large would not necessarily improve the efficiency of majoritarian decision making. Aggregate relative price neutrality ameliorates these problems only in the case in which the apportionment of government revenues to particular services is taken as given. In this last case, supplier incentives to lobby for (proportional) increases in the output of government services would be absent.

In a broad range of cases, there is no trade-off between generality and ordinary economic efficiency. Relative price neutrality is promoted by widely distributing the largest economical number of production centers about the polity of interest. Such general allocations of production are often cost effective. In many cases, concentrating production at a few locations, or within a few firms, increases the cost of government services because it increases the cost of land, labor, and other relatively immobile factors of production in the region surrounding the site of production. Distributing production of such services more uniformly throughout a government's jurisdiction reduces relative prices effects and, at the same time, increases the political efficiency with which government services are selected. Moreover, generality in production tends to increase competition in the relevant markets. Service-by-service price neutrality in many, if not most, areas of government service is as easy to achieve as aggregate price neutrality insofar as decentralized production does not increase production costs.

On the other hand, there are cases in which locational economies are substantial and/or in which the market for a good or service is too small to support more than a handful of efficiently sized firms. Exclusive contracts in some cases may significantly reduce transactions costs. Although not all such "economies" reduce ordinary production costs, as concentrated production tends to promote the formation of "unnatural" monopolies with greater production costs in the long run, it must be acknowledged that there are cases in which concentrated production yields significant economies as in the case of "best shot" technologies (Cornes and Sandler, 1996). This might be said, for example, of the manufacture and servicing of submarines, the example noted earlier. In cases in which the trade-offs are significant, one can easily imagine settings in which all voters prefer low-cost concentrated production to more costly alternatives, although they will, of course, disagree about the "most advantageous" locus of production insofar as specific communities gain (or lose) from securing the production site.

Even in such cases, the institutions of fiscal choice may be constructed in a way to preserve the efficiencies of the generality norm. One method might introduce more generality by "packaging" many goods-and-services decisions into one legislative action dimension. Another familiar method involves delegation of authority to a commission of "experts" whose opinions are not well-known beforehand. Another might involve the introduction of random or lottery-like selection among specific options. (See Chapter 12 for more on this.)

D. Political efficiency and the financing of public goods

Determining the output of a public good or service to be produced and distributed remains problematic until a method of finance is specified. In order to facilitate discussion, traditional analyses of public goods separate issues of taxation from those of efficiency in supply in order to facilitate discussion. (The exception is the so-called *voluntary exchange theory of public finance* [Buchanan, 1949, 1976].) The traditional approach does not examine the institutional structure through which voters, interest groups, and politicians finally make fiscal decisions. In the absence of program benefits, the optimal tax is zero from the vantage point of the electorate in total and any member thereof. If government services confer no benefits, there should be no tax costs (Wicksell, 1896; Wicksell in Musgrave and Peacock, eds., 1967). In the setting in which tax burden is exogenous and not affected by the level of service, additional program services will be desired to the point of satiety. On the other hand, interest groups or dominant coalitions may prefer positive and unequal taxes even in cases in which no services are provided if they secure economic or political advantage from imposing burdens on others in the polity of interest.

Any fixed apportionment of the costs of government services allows a voter's preferred budgetary level to be conceptually defined. Analysis is clearly simpler in the case in which the service is produced and distributed in accordance with generality, but it is possible under other distributional schemes as well. Many different apportionments of the costs of government programs are consistent with economic efficiency, although only a subset of these is consistent with the generality principle, as previously discussed in Chapter 8. Applying the generality rule to methods of taxation increases political efficiency by reducing opportunities for electoral cycles and coalitional conflict over cost shares.

Many relevant properties of methods for sharing the costs of public goods can be analyzed by considering a two-person setting in which a policy decision is to be made over cost shares and output levels for a pure public good (Lindahl, 1919; Lindahl in Musgrave and Peacock, eds., 1967). As A's cost share, α, increases, B's cost share, β, necessarily decreases because the sum of their shares must equal one. Use of this relationship allows us to characterize the payoffs realized by both players in a two-dimensional table (Table 10.1) with A's cost share varying along the left (vertically) and service output varying along the top (horizontally).

Our analysis focuses on two such tables. The good or service level under analysis is assumed to be either a pure public good in the technological sense or a partitionable good or service that is distributed in accordance with the generality principle. The

Table 10.1. *Payoffs to alternative cost shares and output levels under fiscal symmetry*

α	β	$Q = 0$	$Q = 1$	$Q = 2$	$Q = 3$	$Q = 4$
$\alpha = 1,$	$\beta = 0$	0, 0	0, 4	1, 5	−2, 6	−5, 7
$\alpha = 0.75,$	$\beta = 0.25$	0, 0	1, 3	2, 4	0, 4	−2, 4
$\alpha = 0.50,$	$\beta = 0.50$	0, 0	2, 2	3, 3	2, 2	1, 1
$\alpha = 0.25,$	$\beta = 0.75$	0, 0	3, 1	4, 2	4, 0	4, −2
$\alpha = 0,$	$\beta = 1$	0, 0	4, 0	5, 1	6, −2	7, −5

Table 10.2. *Payoffs to alternative cost shares and output levels under fiscal asymmetry*

α	β	$Q = 0$	$Q = 1$	$Q = 2$	$Q = 3$	$Q = 4$
$\alpha = 1,$	$\beta = 0$	0, 0	0, 4	1, 5	−2, 9	−5, 10
$\alpha = 0.75,$	$\beta = 0.25$	0, 0	1, 3	2, 4	0, 7	−2, 7
$\alpha = 0.50,$	$\beta = 0.50$	0, 0	2, 2	3, 3	2, 5	1, 4
$\alpha = 0.25,$	$\beta = 0.75$	0, 0	3, 1	4, 2	4, 3	4, 1
$\alpha = 0,$	$\beta = 1$	0, 0	4, 0	5, 1	6, −1	7, −2

first table lists payoffs in the case in which the players receive identical benefits from the public service. The second table (Table 10.2) represents one in which the benefits received from the government service differs for the two representative individuals. Maximal payoffs are obtained for A along the bottom row of each table where his cost share is zero and for B along the top row where A pays the full cost of the public good. The sum of the payoffs in each column is assumed to be the same, as consistent with the Samuelsonian analysis in which cost shares do not affect the efficiency of the provision of a pure public good. This assumption is not necessary for our analysis but serves as a familiar and tractable point of departure.

We first focus on the symmetric fiscal setting illustrated in Table 10.1. A's maximum payoff occurs in the bottom right-hand corner of the table, and B's occurs in the upper right-hand corner of the table. In a setting in which a majoritarian cycle shifts power between A and B, we would observe a stable government service level of four units of output, but an alternating assignment of tax burden with those out of power bearing the full cost of the public service. In the case in which A and B are equally likely to be in office, each party's average payoff is positive at one unit.

The generality principle applied to cost shares implies that A and B should pay the same cost share for public services. In the numerical example, this requires $\alpha = \beta = 0.5$. If output decisions are predicated on equal cost shares, both parties would choose an output of two units. Note that at two units of output, each receives a payoff of three that dominates the average payoff of one obtained under the evenly rotating majority cycle. The generality principle yields a political choice that is, in this case, Pareto superior to the original unconstrained setting $(3 > 1)$, and the outcome is politically stable.

We now turn to the more problematic case in which the demand for public services differs for the parties in question. For purposes of illustration, we now assume that B has a greater demand for the public service in question than A does over part of the range of interest. B may be prepared to pay more because the service is more productive, because he has higher income, or because he has a relatively stronger personal evaluation of the service in question. A modest change in the payoffs of Table 10.1 is sufficient to illustrate some of the properties of such asymmetric cases. We add three units to the payoffs of B in the last two columns to make Table 10.2. This transformation preserves many of the properties of the symmetric game while introducing relevant asymmetries. A rotating cycle of power between A and B again implies a stable service level of four units of output and a fluctuating assignment of tax burden. Expected payoffs in the numerical illustration are one unit for A and four units for B in the evenly rotating majoritarian cycle.

Note that in this case, restricting those in authority to use equal cost shares fails to achieve either political stability or idealized efficiency. When constrained by an equal cost-sharing rule, A chooses a service level of two units of output when in power, whereas B chooses a service level of three units of output. Unconstrained majoritarian rotation will generate payoffs of $[0.5(7-5)]$, equals 1, for A and $[0.5(10-2)]$, equals 4, for B. By comparison, majoritarian rotation under generality would generate payoffs of $[0.5(3+2)]$, equals 2.5, for A and $[0.5(3+5)]$, equals 4, for B, a composite result that is Pareto superior.

In the asymmetric case, stability and efficiency can only be assured by setting cost shares equal to marginal benefit shares, that is to say, by using Lindahl prices. Lindahl cost shares set net marginal benefits equal to zero at the chosen output level. In the case represented, this assignment occurs where $\alpha = 0.25$ and $\beta = 0.75$ at an output of three units. (Note that A's marginal benefits exactly equal his marginal tax cost at an output of three units. At this output, a one-unit change in output does not increase A's net benefits. B's marginal benefits also are approximately equal to his marginal cost in that any change in output level reduces B's net benefits – at $Q = 3$, $\alpha = 0.25$, and $\beta = 0.75$.) Faced by Lindahl prices imposed "constitutionally," B would choose three units of output, and A would have no incentive to change that output when he comes to power.

Lindahl cost shares are inherently unequal in cases in which those served are willing to pay more or less at the margin for the service received. It is clear that Lindahl taxes violate the generality norm. It is also clear, however, that the stylized efficiency promised by the levy of Lindahl tax prices would not be generated by any nonconstrained majority coalition. In the two-person illustration, as noted earlier, majority solutions will rotate between the upper and lower right-hand cells in Table 10.2. Recognition of the reality of majoritarian politics suggests that, even in settings in which demands for the commonly shared good or service differ, enforcement of a generality constraint may, in net, be more efficient than unconstrained majoritarian rotation.

In a more realistic political setting, the practical difficulty with Lindahl taxes is that benefits are inherently subjective and difficult to estimate. Reasonable estimates are clearly problematic in cases in which benefits differ among individuals and are not strongly correlated with readily observable measures such as use rates, income, or distance from point of service. In cases in which a consensus about the best objective correlate does not exist, for whatever reason, significant conflict among groups is likely to occur as estimation methods are debated with fiscal advantage in mind. Estimates of benefits become arbitrary and fluctuate as different groups achieve political power. In these settings, benefit taxes may be said to be, themselves, politically infeasible. Less than ideal general taxes on a broad objective tax base may yield better results than politicized benefit taxes.

The analysis of Chapter 8 suggests that in cases in which every individual in the polity of interest receives every service provided by the government, a broad-based tax with a uniform rate earmarked to specific services can increase political stability. In such cases, everyone shares in the cost of providing the service and all would judge the service on the basis of costs and benefits received. On the other hand, many alternative broad tax bases share this property. Generality does not, by itself, uniquely determine the best tax base.

E. Conclusion and summary

The manner in which public services should be distributed and financed have long been issues at the core of public economics. The literature that has emerged addresses a variety of questions about the optimal level of provision and methods by which such goods should be financed. Less attention has been focused on the process by which public service decisions are actually made or in the manner by which such choices could be improved. Analysis of political decision making clearly requires an understanding of distributional aspects of public production and finance but also of the channels by which levels of provision can be influenced by politically active individuals. Such an analysis requires that the demand and supply of government services be analyzed in conjunction with the political institutions under which fiscal policy choices will be made.

Distributive aspects of the supply of public services have effects on the political demands for those services. Application of the generality principle to the production, distribution, and financing of those services reduces the range of distributional conflict that occurs and thereby increases political efficiency. In this sense there may be said to be no trade-off between equity and efficiency at the constitutional level of politics. Other rules for apportioning services might serve this end as well. Distributing services according to age or race or zodiac sign would also reduce fiscal conflict and thereby increase political efficiency. However, these distributional rules would not be as broadly acceptable as the ones implied by the generality principle. Our demonstration of the efficiency of the generality principle has been based on the improved welfare of all relevant parties. Other distributional rules would garner less widespread support because nongeneral rules would only infrequently increase each person's welfare over the unconstrained case.

It might be argued that uniformity in the distribution of publicly supplied goods and services is an impossibility. After all, any service that is uniformly provided in some sense will be unequal in another as long as people and circumstances differ. For example, equal availability implies different subjective benefit levels unless all users are homogeneous. However, only to the extent that benefits have measurable correlates, such as objectively measurable flows of service or monetary net advantage, can more generality be distinguished from less generality. It is for this reason that we have focused on objective service levels in the analysis of this chapter. The political efficiency associated with the generality principle arises because of effects of uniform service provision on incentives for political action in these cases.

If our argument about the general appeal of the generality principle with regard to the provision of public services has validity, we should, in practice, observe widespread adherence to such principles in government finance. We do observe that many public services are distributed and financed with rough accordance to the generality principle. However, deviations from generality remain significant. The presence of narrow industrial, labor, and regional lobbying groups implies that the level of generality is imperfect. Although the broad outlines of budgetary policy may largely conform with the generality principle, the specific details evidently do not. The tax code continues to treat different kinds of income differently, and many public goods and services are produced and distributed in a far less than uniform fashion. The manner in which, for example, public capital projects are produced and distributed seems to reflect the effective political power of regional representatives more than the generality principle. Political efficiency could be further improved by greater deference to the generality principle.

11 Generality and redistribution

In Chapter 10 we examined how the generality principle might be applied to constrain the productive state. In this chapter we examine the majoritarian politics of the transfer state. Here the role of government is not always so evident as in arguments supporting the production of public goods. Generality, narrowly conceived, cannot really apply to the transfer state insofar as transfers, by definition, involve unequal treatment in the sense that transfers imply the existence of net taxpayers and net transfer recipients. On the other hand, transfer programs can be more or less general and can run more or less afoul of the political inefficiencies associated with nongeneral programs. Can an argument comparable to that developed in support of general taxation and the production of public services be made to the effect that the generality norm should be extended to the transfer side of the fiscal account? And what would generality mean in this context? What is the transfer side equivalent of the flat-rate income tax? And, given the possible constitutional enforcement of generality, could the modern welfare-transfer state remain both majoritarian in its politics and viable in its economics? Or does the welfare-transfer state depend for its very survival on discriminatory departures from any generality principle?

We propose to analyze the working of majoritarian politics in a constitutional setting that allows government spending that is not limited to the financing of public goods but is directed explicitly to particular individuals and groups in the form of monetary transfers.

A. Transfers

The institutions of the welfare state are familiar, and they are roughly comparable over the separate polities of most Western nations. Without exception, governments spend large shares on their budgets on transfers to the old – institutional arrangements that meet some, but not all, of the criteria for generality. Beyond transfers to the aged, welfare states extend transfers to the disabled, the poor, children, and, more directly, make categorical disbursements to subsidize specific partitionable services such as medical care and education.

The essential point to be made here, before examining separate categories of outlay, is that there is no direct publicness involved, at least in the technological sense. A monetary transfer to an old person is aimed directly at providing that person with purchasing power. There is no explicit spillover or shared benefit beyond the shared altruistic impulse of fellow citizens; rivalry rather than nonrivalry in consumption is an explicit part of the institutional package. In making transfers to the aged, as well as those made for other welfare programs, government is using tax revenues, whether these are raised from general or particular levies, to finance privately partitionable benefits to persons who are politically determined to be eligible. It is clear that distributional conflict emerges as a potentially disruptive element here – conflict that is sublimated or even nonexistent when genuinely public goods, technologically defined, are tax financed. Refer to the classic example of national defense outlay. Conflict may arise over the distribution of tax shares, but conflict does not arise over the sharing of the benefits of security, as such. The welfare state, in its very nature, and independently of political decision rules, embodies the potential for greater distributional conflict than the productive state, which is limited to the financing of collective consumption or nonrival goods and services.

As we have stressed earlier, the generality principle, applied as a constitutional constraint, offers one means of reducing the range of politically driven distributional discrimination in a regime of majoritarian politics. As outlined in the previous chapters in Part III, uniformly distributed general financing of government services enhances political efficiency. But how would a comparable generality constraint work for a regime of explicit transfers?

B. Redistributive limits in a stylized median voter model[1]

Consider a stylized setting in which government collects a fixed revenue total from taxes, whether general or specific. This total is, let us say, earmarked for welfare state outlay; none is to be allocated for spending to finance productive or protective state services. How might this revenue total be distributed among persons so as to minimize the potential for political exploitation and for investment in political rent seeking? Put in this way, the question seems to be answered by equal-per-head transfer payments (demogrants). In effect, this idealized transfer scheme converts the inclusive fiscal arrangement into an analog that involves the tax financing of a nonrival good or service.

A flat rate of tax on all income combined with a set of equal-per-head demogrants would perhaps come closest to meeting the generality criterion while implementing redistribution through the fiscal process. Distributional conflict would remain in that high-income recipients would prefer a relatively low tax rate, whereas low-income recipients would prefer a relatively high rate. But in the context of our earlier models, the alternatives would all lie "along the diagonal," and we should expect, in this case, that voter preferences would be single peaked. The preferences of the median voter (or class) would be decisive in the choice among alternative fiscal outcomes, each one of which would meet the generality criterion.

How large would the transfer budget be in the stylized median voter model in which a flat-rate income tax finances equal-per-head demogrants? In order to get at an answer here, even conceptually, other parameters must be specified. We restrict the model further by postulating that persons (voters) differ among themselves only in incomes. Specifically, we eliminate age differences, which become relevant later as we examine old-age transfers. How high will the flat-rate (proportional) tax be, as chosen by the effective majority coalition?

The maximand is the posttax, posttransfer income for the median voter. Because the median pretax income is likely to be lower than the pretax mean income, we should predict that the rate of tax will be positive; some redistributive transfers will be put in place. The median voter, in this case, will expect to get back more in transfers than she pays in tax. How much more will depend on both the structure of the pretax income distribution and the patterns of adjustment to the tax–transfer process. If there are no behavioral adjustments at all, to either taxes or transfers, if there is no leakage in the transfer process, and if the median income is lower than average income, the median voter's posttax income is maximized by the imposition of a 100 percent rate of tax. All income in the polity would be collected in taxes and all returned to persons as demogrants.

Behavioral adjustments will, of course, occur, and, further, any redistributive program will involve leakages. If the median voter ignores the behavioral reaction that she, herself, makes to the tax and transfer, she will, quite simply, choose that rate of tax that will maximize revenue intake, again ignoring leakages. When she recognizes that her own utility will be impacted negatively by the tax and that there will be some leakage, a rate of tax somewhat lower than the revenue maximizing rate will be chosen.

Several other attenuating factors may enter the calculus to place upper limits on the tax rate. The effective time horizon that informs choice may be relevant. Present-value revenue maximization will suggest a lower rate of tax than current-period maximization to the extent that the tax, in itself, is predicted to impact on capital formation (Buchanan and Lee, 1982). The median voter may also intuitively recognize that the possible presence of economy-wide increasing returns will cause the tax to exert negative effects on the aggregate rate of growth (Buchanan and Yoon, 1995). An additional tempering element in the median voter's choice may arise from considerations of predicted mobility among income classes. If a person anticipates that her own income level in later periods may exceed median income levels, she may be reluctant to choose relatively high rates of tax if there is any expectation that, once established and put in place, high rates of tax will become quasi-permanent. For these, and possibly for a variety of other reasons, the rate of tax, if generally imposed on all incomes under the conditions postulated, would seem likely to fall well below that rate that would maximize revenue.

The political competition between the public goods or productive sector of the budget and the welfare-transfer sector should also be emphasized. The median voter who explicitly uses the fisc as a means of maximizing posttax, posttransfer income is likely to exhibit bias in favor of transfers over public goods financing, even if the generality norm is in place (Flowers and Danzon, 1984). The inclusive budget will tend to be relatively small in its financing of genuinely public goods and relatively large in its financing of direct transfers. (This pattern of outlay seems to be characteristic of the United States experience in the late twentieth century. There is a widespread sense that governmental outlay on "social overhead capital" has been "too low," while politically popular transfer spending has grown "too rapidly.")

C. Pressures for nongenerality

The discussion in the preceding section was aimed at making some conceptual predictions as to the size of the transfer budget in a regime in which the generality principle operates on both the tax and transfer sides of the fiscal account. Even within this unrealistic set of restrictions, majoritarian democracy is likely to generate a relatively large transfer budget, and one that will reduce, perhaps substantially, the rate of aggregate economic growth in the economy. Such a fiscal system, if it ever could be realized in practice, even to some very rough approximation, would set in motion strong arguments in support of reductions in the size of the transfer budget. Quite apart from the possible negative effects on aggregate economic growth, critics would suggest that the generality imposed on one or both sides of the fiscal account tends to run counter to the very purpose and meaning of the welfare state. The arguments that might be adduced in support of the generality norm are unlikely to be convincing. Such arguments would suggest the vulnerability of any idealized pattern of welfare transfers to the machinations of majoritarian politics. The differentiation emergent from such politics is not likely to match that which might be deemed desirable by nonpolitical criteria.

If a demogrant structure should be in place, advocates of reform could point directly to the apparently useless circulation of payments that would be involved in payments to above-median income voters–taxpayers. Why should high-income recipients, who pay proportionally higher taxes under the flat-rate scheme, get back, through demogrants, some share of their tax payments? Surely, so the argument might go, this element of the inclusive tax–transfer process is wasteful. If there are leakages and behavioral adjustments to either taxes or transfers thereby creating excess burdens, *all* persons in the economy can be made better off by a carefully designed departure from generality. If high-income recipients are eliminated from the demogrant rolls, the rate of tax on income can be lowered sufficiently to make such persons better off, while median and lower income persons, who continue to receive transfers, can be made better off through somewhat higher transfer payments. The situation sets up a clear example in which a genuinely Pareto-superior change is possible – the introduction of a means test for transfer eligibility along with some reduction in tax rate and an increase in transfers to those who remain eligible. Political economists who are trained in the elementary logic of the Pareto criterion would surely offer supporting counsel for such reform.

We should have here a real-world example of the Pareto superiority of an off-diagonal position, compared with one on the diagonal. The argument against any such reform can be made only on the basis of understanding the elementary logic of majoritarian politics. Once this understanding is allowed to enter the discourse, the standard Pareto construction becomes irrelevant. The Pareto-superior outcome that seems so attractive is not feasible politically because it is dominated, for the decisive majority as reflected in the preferences of the median voter, by a different outcome that may involve means testing for transfers, but in which there is an unchanged or *increased* rate of tax along with increases in the size of transfers to recipients who remain eligible. Clearly, this change politically dominates the suggested Pareto-superior change that might be advocated by the neutral political economist. The actual change that the majority would put in place makes the persons whose demogrants are eliminated by the means test substantially worse off.

The more general political implication is clear. Any introduction of means testing, as an explicitly selected departure from generality in defining eligibility for transfers, creates incentives for majoritarian cycles, and rent seeking as policies more favorable to those members of majority coalitions are pursued. Any promise of tax rate reductions, and of reduced budgetary size, should be treated as siren songs by those who are not members of the political majority. Any change that introduces separate criteria for eligibility offers incentives for political rent seeking aimed both at preventing adverse discrimination and promoting favorable discrimination.

If some citizens–taxpayers are to be declared ineligible, where is the line to be drawn? And are there additional departures from the generality norm that may be justified? Political inefficiency emerges in any setting in which individuals and groups are encouraged to consider themselves subjects or objects of politically induced exploitation. Any existing sense of political community is necessarily eroded.

It is interesting to contrast two possible sources for departures from the generality embodied in a flat-tax, equal-per-head demogrant setting. We have discussed the pressures for means testing to restrict eligibility for receipt of transfer payments. Pressures may also arise to eliminate (or not to include in the first place) persons at the low end of the income scale from tax liability. Why should a person be subjected to the same flat rate of tax on her income when she will get back, in transfer payments, a much larger sum? Is not such fiscal circulation unnecessary and surely wasteful?

Note that the impetus for such a change is not as likely to arise from the median voter, or her representative, as is the case with means testing for upper income persons. The median voter whose maximand is the net transfer, at least in the stylized model considered here, will oppose any reduction in tax liability because any such action would reduce revenues available for distribution and, hence, her own demogrant. A more complex "bundle" may, of course, be worked out in which low income persons are shifted off the tax rolls while, their transfers are selectively cut back (a reverse means test), thereby ensuring that the position of the median voter remains unaffected or even possibly improved. As in the straightforward means testing example, however, any such reform is majority dominated by an alternative that simply cuts payments to the low-income persons in a discriminatory fashion.

D. Public and private demand for transfers

As the last example indicates, however, and, as we noted earlier, the modern welfare state, even in its overextended variants, is not described accurately by the stylized models of majoritarian exploitation. These models retain their usefulness, however, in allowing us to isolate tendencies that are always present, even if other elements seem to dominate the institutional reality that we observe. The redistributive activities of the welfare state tend to be justified under a rhetoric of public interest, in which the transfer programs are alleged to be generally beneficial to *all* members of the political community.

Consider general tax financing of transfers to the poor; that is, to persons and families that qualify as recipients through some criteria that measure pretransfer income and/or wealth. Empirically, it is evident that transfers to the poor are desired by many persons who are not poor. Their utilities are increased by collective transfers to the poor (Hochman and Rodgers, 1969). In a majoritarian setting in which the voting franchise is limited to those who pay net taxes, a scheme of fiscal transfers would be generated that would reflect roughly the median preferences of those persons who do not become eligible for receipt of transfers. In such a setting, the fiscal alternatives would indeed lie along the diagonal, in terms of our earlier analyses, because the redistribution would be a public good available equally to all those who remain outside the recipient group.

In a setting in which the franchise is not so limited, however, and in which, specifically, those who expect to be transfer recipients are themselves voters, the political decision structure is dramatically modified. A direct conflict of interest is created between those who seek transfers to themselves, as privately measured monetary values at their disposal, and those who must finance these transfers through taxes. This conflict is present quite independently of any desire that taxpayers may exhibit in support of poverty relief. Stable majoritarian politics, under universal franchise, must work to extend levels of transfer beyond those that reflect the median preferences of nonrecipients. Recipient demands for transfers remain nonsatiated over the whole range of feasible options. Consequently, the median transfer desired by the general electorate necessarily is greater than that desired by altruistic nonrecipients. As the population of recipients increases relative to that of nonrecipients, majoritarian politics tends to shift transfer levels further from those acceptable to net taxpayers, thereby exacerbating political tension and increasing the potential for class conflict.

As noted earlier, some of these same pressures will exist even under the flat-tax, equal-demogrant scheme. What the general scheme would eliminate are incentives for investment in efforts to qualify for transfers under separate and differential fiscal treatment for this or that group that might claim "entitlement" under some public interest argument.

E. General fiscal transfers to the old

Without exception, modern welfare states implement massive fiscal transfers from currently productive members of the political community to persons who have retired from employment. In one sense, this differential treatment of a particular class of persons represents a clear departure from any principle of generality. Members of this one group are singled out for differentially favored fiscal treatment; the observed outcomes seems to lie off the diagonal.

In another sense, however, the generality criterion is satisfied. Because all persons get old, all persons are eventually eligible for program benefits. Only death denies members of the polity the ultimate status in which they might qualify for eligibility for transfers. In this feature, therefore, the wasteful rent seeking that welfare state transfers encourage through the establishment of other classificatory boundaries does not arise with retirement support schemes, per se. On the other hand, conflict between transfer recipients and net taxpayers remains, thereby potentially reducing attitudes of commonality in collective action.

Our previous analysis of redistribution to the poor provides some guidance about how a general public pension plan might be designed. An age-conditioned demogrant program would have properties that parallel those of the untargeted program discussed previously. Indeed, if one ignores the economic and political effects of the delay between the time of tax payment and the receipt of transfers, the programs would be essentially identical. Generality assures that policy parameters lie along the diagonal and that median voter results tend to occur. In this sense, the generality principle may be said to be satisfied with a pension system based on a broad-based negative income tax. Transfers aimed at securing maximal lifetime personal income for the median voter, again, are constrained by a variety of incentive effects of the tax and transfer system. Tax rates and program benefits will be extended only to the point where the expected marginal increase in median voter wealth equals marginal tax cost. Altruistic aims tend to increase transfers above those that would be required to maximize the median voter's net income insofar as the aged are, for whatever reason, deemed worthy of charity.

The delay between tax payment and transfer receipt introduces several new features to the previous analysis. In the case of an ordinary negative income tax, the median voter chooses program parameters and benefits immediately from them. Moreover, any eligibility restrictions that might be contemplated will not exclude the median voter, herself, from a contemporaneous transfer program if her aim is at least partly nonaltruistic. However, in the case of a "guaranteed" public pension, restricting the pool of beneficiaries by setting an age qualification *above* the current age of the present median voter can potentially secure greater transfers for the current median voter insofar as reduced tax rates encourage more rapid economic growth and a larger future taxable base. The incentive effects of higher taxes and subsidies are generally acknowledged to be larger in the long run than in the short run. In effect, the present value of tax receipts per eligible person increases as the pool of currently eligible recipients shrinks and economic growth occurs.

Of course, the "guarantee" of an age-linked demogrant program depends upon its continued political viability. Insofar as the current median voter is not herself a current beneficiary of the program, the personally relevant parameters of this program will be established independently by a future median voter at the time that the current median voter reaches the age of eligibility. Current "commitments" or constitutional provisions are always subject to amendment by future majorities. So long as the current median voter expects to benefit from the existing program, she will continue or expand it, even if younger or wealthier voters do increasingly less well (Browning, 1975). If eliminating or curtailing the program appears to shrink the present value of costs more than future benefits for the median voter, the public pension program will be reduced or eliminated.

The political dilemma facing the current median voter, in a stable democracy not constrained by an intertemporal generality principle, is predicting the inclinations of successive median voters, especially those who will control program benefits and taxes after the median voter's retirement. As the median voter become older, as the population as a whole ages, or as medical progress increases longevity, program benefits will tend to rise; and as current program benefit levels become more costly to provide, program benefits for those currently eligible will tend to fall. Population dynamics and technological improvements induce fluctuations in tax rates and payments received by successive generations (Congleton and Shughart, 1990).

Adherence to the generality principle increases the political viability of public pension programs by sharply reducing the scope for amending program benefits and tax structures. Recall the sense in which a public pension program in general is analogous to the manner in which a negative income tax is general. All persons should face the same marginal tax rate (which implies identical taxes on holdings of productive inputs) and receive the same age-related demogrant, adjusted for variation in purchasing power. Alternatively, interpreted as a forced saving scheme, return payments related uniformly to prior tax payments would also meet the generality criteria. Intertemporal programs have to ensure equal treatment through time if they are to satisfy the generality principle. This implies that, once enacted, essentially they become permanent.

F. Transfers to other targeted groups

Transfers to groups in which the membership is well-known to be noninclusive differ systematically from those of demogrant programs in which all citizens currently qualify or share expectations of qualifying for programs. In such programs, eligibility is determined by politically chosen, but not politically defined, criteria. Eligibility itself becomes a coalition cleaving issue that may attract significant political investment by the groups that will be affected by the criteria developed. Examples include payments to qualifying persons who currently are physically or mentally handicapped in specific ways, or, more generally, persons who, for various reasons, are unable to earn incomes. As in generalized transfer programs, if members of net recipient groups possess the voting franchise, direct politicization of the transfer system within ordinary majoritarian politics must set up direct conflicts of interest between potential claimants and net taxpayers who must be called on to finance the transfers.

Any program of differential support necessarily makes the relevant selection criteria the principal determinant of net benefit levels. As benefit levels for those qualifying are limited by the size of the receipts from those excluded from the program and the apportionment of benefits among those included, there will be a tendency to minimize the size of the recipient group, although at some risk of coalitional instability. Because all excluded parties are net taxpayers and only included parties can be net-benefit recipients, every group has a clear incentive to seek inclusion. Those excluded from program benefits are naturally willing to join any coalition that offers reduced overall expenditures or, better still, redefines eligibility so that they acquire net benefits from the program. Insofar as the latter tends to increase generality, this is all to the good. However, as one form of discrimination is substituted for another, such programs suffer from all of the usual political problems of dividing-the-pie games.

Another significant feature distinguishes many discriminatory transfer programs from generalized programs. To the extent that eligibility for transfer payments depends in any way on the behavior of prospective claimants, the moral hazard of the familiar sort emerges and opens up possibilities for abuse that are absent in an old-age pension scheme. Consider programs that finance transfers to persons who are disabled. Clearly, these programs are vulnerable to bogus claims of disability. Rent-seeking investment in validating claims for eligibility becomes profitable, quite apart from the direct conflict of interest between recipients and net taxpayers. (In the United States, many persons classified as legally blind simultaneously are reported to hold valid licenses to drive automobiles. Persons who are eligible for child support payments have a standing incentive to produce children. Incentive effects of the aid to dependent children [AFDC] program is often cited as a major cause of dependency in the underclass in modern American cities.)

G. In-kind provision or subsidization for particular services

The basic analysis also applies to those elements of the modern welfare state that involve either direct provision or subsidization of particular services to members of differentially selected groups rather than direct monetary transfers. The example that comes to mind is medical care, which is either directly provided or subsidized in almost all countries. The economic inefficiencies associated with in-kind redistribution are well-known, but these are not our focus of interest here, which is political efficiency rather than economic efficiency, as such. The additional feature that warrants notice, and which relates to all such in-kind programs, stems from the potential for producer rents that may be anticipated by persons and groups in the industries that supply the designated services – rents that will, in turn, create conflicts of political interest over and beyond those between prospective beneficiaries and net taxpayers. Prospective suppliers may join with prospective beneficiaries in support of extensions in the size and scope of in-kind transfers, even if such suppliers may, at the same time, remain net taxpayers.

As in the other cases discussed previously, genuine constitutionalization of all such in-kind programs can be helpful in attenuating the potential distributional conflict. But as the programs themselves depart further from generality (as the margins for behavioral adjustment increase), the difficulties of thinking of such programs in constitutional terms increase, perhaps exponentially.

H. Some difficulties of constitutional fiscal discrimination

As we have stressed throughout this book, we must look more carefully at the operation of majoritarian politics and at prospects for imposing constitutional constraints on this operation. Any group, in which the members are both granted the voting franchise and made eligible for differentially favorable fiscal treatment, will seek to advance its own interests through majoritarian politics, and any such behavior will be interpreted to be fiscal exploitation by persons who are net taxpayers. By definition here, we cannot think of imposing the generality requirement in its inclusive sense because the very purpose of a discriminatory transfer scheme is to finance transfers to a designated class of beneficiaries. How, then, can a discriminatory transfer scheme be made politically viable within the abstract environment explored in this book?

At this point, it is essential that the categorical distinction between choices among constitutional rules or constraints and choices made by legislative coalitions within the set of constitutional constraints that exist be recognized. Majority coalitions must be restricted in their authority to advance the interests of some groups differentially at the costs of other groups. If the inclusive generality constraint fails here, a more specific constraint may prove necessary. If all income transfer programs adopted by normal legislation must satisfy the generality principle, differential fiscal treatment among members of defined groups must be *constitutionally* chosen and put in place and thereby exempted from the strictures of the generality norm. A somewhat different, and summary, way of putting the point here is to say that a constitutional welfare state might be politically viable, whereas a majoritarian welfare state is not.

The difficulty with a constitutional welfare state is best illustrated with reference to the social security systems in place throughout the world, although the argument can be extended readily to other programs. As noted, all persons grow old; hence, all members of the political community must ultimately become eligible for receipt of transfers, if the only criterion is age itself. From this fact it follows that all persons may, at least conceptually, enter as *equals* in a political dialogue concerning levels of fiscal support that are to be collectively provided to the old. In an idealized setting, each person would be allowed to participate in the constitutional choice process only once, presumably at the onset of the income-earning period. In reality, of course, constitutional choices must be made under open franchise in which all persons participate. The system to be chosen must be put in place at a discrete point in time, but under the generalized understanding that, once chosen and in place, the system will remain quasi-permanent and hence immune from period-to-period manipulation due to shifting majority coalitions. In this sense, constitutionalization implies that the transfer system, once chosen, is appropriately treated as "off the table" for the interplay of ordinary majoritarian politics.

However, modern welfare states find themselves in fiscal crises because programs of retirement income support have been put in place that are not internally consistent with the transfer claims made upon them and the tax rates designed to finance such claims. Consider a familiar setting in which citizens, acting through their legislative representatives, introduce a pay-as-we-go structure of retirement income support and, at the same time, recognize this structure to be effectively constitutional and immune from period-to-period distributional conflict. Any viable fiscal structure must incorporate some recognition of the interdependence between the preferred level of retirement income support, relative to preretirement income, and the tax rates required to finance such support, which, in turn, depends on the ratio between the number of preretirement income earners (the net taxpayers) and the number of prospective retirees. This ratio is critical because it determines the rate of tax that is necessary to support any specified level of pension transfers. It becomes impossible, therefore, to constitutionalize the level of retirement income support and, at the same time, the rate of tax on productive income earners when, as, and if the age profile of the citizenry shifts over time in unexpected ways.

Any such shifts make reforms or changes in the structure necessary, and, when any such changes are discussed, the vulnerability to majoritarian distributional conflict emerges. Effective constitutionalization would suggest that tax rates (or age for eligibility) move upward if the ratio tilts unexpectedly toward a higher number of prospective retirees because of increased life expectancy and that transfer payments move downward if the ratio tilts because of declines in birth rates. Such a rule would violate intergenerational generality but would preserve the fiscal viability of the public pension system.

In reality, old-age pension systems in modern democracies, even if they may have been established to reflect some rough approximation of median constitutional preferences, have become politicized, or "deconstitutionalized," as anticipated entitlements and tax rates become inconsistent and place pressures on political coalitions. The generality norm, which may have been honored indirectly when the systems were initially constructed, loses significance as the conflict between current taxpayers and current transfer recipients moves to center stage. At this stage, means testing becomes politically attractive because it reduces the financial claims on the system. Little attention is paid to the violation of the generality principle under which the system was established. And, once the system becomes directly politicized, the whole structure becomes vulnerable to majoritarian manipulation.

Formal constitutionalization of this and other aspects of the welfare payment structure can attenuate potential political conflict through requirements of lengthy amending procedures and super majorities. In cases in which the basic criteria for eligibility are set constitutionally rather than as ordinary legislation, and behavioral adjustments are not sufficient to erode the very meaning of such criteria, the discriminatory structure of these programs may remain viable. If, however, behavioral adjustments are such that what might have been roughly the constitutional preferences of the median voter are grossly distorted, and if the structure is successfully "gamed" so that ever-increasing burdens are placed on taxpayers, some continuing reassessment of the system may be necessary. In any such reassessment, a constitutional, rather than a majoritarian, perspective will be required.

Although constitutionalization reduces political conflict in areas constitutionalized, it does not fully immunize and isolate those policies from the political competition among separate and potentially rotating majority coalitions that describe ordinary politics. Constitutionalization significantly raises the cost of policy reform by placing a more lengthy and demanding decision process between the status quo and program amendment.

I. Conclusion

As the discussion in the preceding sections has suggested, the extension and application of the generality principle to the transfer sector of the budget may seem, at the outset, to involve a contradiction in terms. Almost by definition, transfer payments, in money or in kind, are specifically directed toward defined subsets of the citizenry. Generality implies equal-per-head transfers (demogrants) or at least equal availability, which may seem to involve useless fiscal circulation to above-median income citizens and to violate the very purpose of the welfare state. It remains, nonetheless, useful to understand the full implications of any departure from such a general structure.

As they are observed to operate in practice, Western welfare states embody massive transfers to the old that have increased substantially through time, clearly introducing a major departure from generality both at every point in time, and through time, as tax rates and benefit levels have increased. Intertemporal generality, as a constitutional principle, would increase the stability of long-term programs in a manner analogous to that which equal treatment period by period increased the policy stability of day-to-day politics. By reducing the scope for permissible policy reforms through time, generality assures both the existence of a current median voter and increased interest in the continuation of intertemporal transfer programs.

Generality, thereby, effectively constitutionalizes intertemporal transfer programs and immunizes them from majoritarian manipulation of outcomes to the differential advantage of members of current dominant coalitions, although, as in other policy areas, it does not eliminate the appeal of such discriminating programs. As it is commonly described, the welfare state that embodies tax-financed transfer payments, in money or in kind to members of defined groups in the population, is compatible with democratic processes only if the structure of the whole transfer sector is maintained in a manner consistent with the generality principle or considered to be a quasi-permanent part of the effective constitution of the polity, and thereby beyond the boundaries of interferences by rotating majority coalitions.

12 Generality without uniformity: Social insurance

To this point, we have argued that government policies should aim at uniformity if they are to conform to the generality principle. Government policies that have uniform consequences for all within a polity obviously meet the requirement. A pure public good is equally available to all within its reach. A proportional tax on a broad base implies uniform marginal and average tax rates. Transfers may take the form of universal demogrants. General laws of property should apply to all within the polity of interest without regard to the geneology, region, age, or wealth of the owner. We have argued that such uniform treatment of individual citizens generally improves political and economic efficiency by reducing coalitional instability and incentives for rent seeking.

In this and the following chapter, we demonstrate that some departures from ex post uniformity may be consistent with our analysis of the political merits of the generality principle. It is well-known that there are many cases in which conventional economic efficiency requires nonuniform service levels insofar as preferences, wealth, or circumstances among persons vary significantly. It may seem troubling, indeed problematic, that the generality principle seems to demand uniformity in settings in which established normative theories of public economics seem to require differential treatment. One can well imagine some cases in which completely uniform policy consequences would fail to command a consensus even from behind an idealized Rawlsian veil. Nonetheless, issues of political efficiency would remain germane.

It bears noting that the benefits of adhering to the generality principle do not require completely uniform service levels in the objective sense that every citizen must be observed to receive exactly the same measured flow of service as any other. The transactions costs of majoritarian politics are reduced so long as institutions preserve ex ante generality for the relevant group of political decision makers. Insofar as the cost of governance can be reduced by adopting institutional devices consistent with the generality principle, even in cases with nonuniform service provision, it can be argued that efficiency concepts have been too narrowly applied in many, if not most, prior analyses that may seem to support differential treatment.

Trade-offs between generality and ordinary economic efficiency often reflect the institutional setting used as the basis of analysis. In this chapter we demonstrate that ex ante stochastic uniformity is sufficient to achieve the political efficiency gains associated with the generality principle.

A. Statistical uniformity: Insurance and lotteries

When individuals purchase a lottery ticket or an insurance policy, they generally acquire a service that is ex ante the same for all parties that make the purchase. Each ticket provides its owner with the same chance of winning the lottery as any other of

129

equal value, and the final prize is the same for whomever holds the winning ticket. Similarly, many equally priced insurance policies provide every insured party with the same ex ante coverage for a particular contingency. Ex post, after the lottery drawing or the calamity occurs, individuals will, of course, receive significantly different payouts. Good or bad luck may be said to vary across purchasers, but not the chance of compensation. It is well-known at the moment of purchase that there will be only a few ticket holders who will win some coveted prize in the case of a lottery. Similarly, it is well-known at the moment an insurance policy is purchased that only a few policyholders will be afflicted by a covered disease or traumatized by accident.

Such impersonal lotteries and insurance schemes satisfy the requirements of the generality principle at the time of purchase, but not at the time of payout. This result is accepted by all who purchase the service – indeed it is this result that makes it feasible for suppliers to offer the services at prices low enough to command the interest of the prospective purchasers.

Many government programs confer stochastic rather than certain benefits on those who ultimately secure benefits from the services furnished. Prior to a fire, a fire department provides services uniformly for all whose houses might catch fire within its service area. After a fire has been reported, the level of service varies dramatically. The direct beneficiaries are those who live at or near properties that actually burn. Similarly, a uniform public pension program provides annual benefits to those who expect to live beyond a given age, but it is clearly advantageous only for those who actually do live beyond the age of eligibility. Tort law provides uniform advantages insofar as it encourages greater precautions to be taken by all potential tort feasors, but only actual tort feasors or victims directly pay or recover damages attributed to improper conduct or accidents.

Some forms of impersonal uncertainty generate uniform expectations at the moment of choice, although they imply nonuniform policy outcomes as the future unfolds. If tastes, including predispositions toward risk, are similar for the citizens of some polity of interest, a fair state lottery or insurance program has actuarially identical benefits for all participants. What is required for the political efficiency properties of generality is that the stochastic process be free from favoritism: sufficiently independent and uniform that ex ante expected service levels are the same for all within the polity of interest.

Not every government program with a stochastic element satisfies the generality principle. A medical insurance program can be designed to favor particular classes of health problems that are not uniformly distributed within the polity. The stochastic provision of some services may similarly favor one group over another insofar as the conditional distribution varies with geographic location, age, income, or other personal characteristics. The probability of receiving, or paying, for a stochastic service can be made to be greater for some groups than for others.

Indeed, the political conflict is potentially greater in the stochastic cases than in their deterministic counterparts, insofar as conflict now includes determination of the appropriate probability distributions or stochastic criteria to be used as the basis of distributing the program services at issue.[1] Conflict over the scale of stochastic programs and their manner of finance and production resembles that of their nonstochastic

Table 12.1. *Alternative probabilistic formulas for distributing program services*

Formula 1	Formula 2	Formula 3	Formula 4	Formula 5
(.35, .55, .10)	(.20, .40, .40)	(.33, .33, .33)	(.40, .20, .40)	(.10, .35, .55)

counterparts. Choosing criteria that are not uniformly distributed across individuals similarly engenders conflict and, potentially, electoral cycles in much the same manner that alternative deterministic apportioning rules promote conflict over ordinary government services.

The problem of coalitional instability induced by probabilistic distributional formulas is illustrated with the numerical example depicted in Table 12.1. Suppose that an exclusive public service, production facility, or block grant is to be granted to one of three individuals, parties, or regions according to some stochastic formula. Five formulas are assumed to be under consideration. Four of them have unequal probability distributions, and one has a uniform distribution. Formula 3 yields an ex ante general program in the sense that it distributes the grant impersonally in accordance with a uniform probability distribution.

Note that each of the nonuniform apportioning probability distributions on the agenda is majority preferred to the uniform result. Formulas 1, 2, 4, and 5 secure majority approval over the uniformly distributed benefits case. The program with the greatest concentration of expected services to a bare majority generally dominates more uniform programs. Thus, (.35, .55, .10) is majority preferred to (.20, .40, .40), which is majority preferred to (.33, .33, .33). Without a restriction on the permitted distributions, an infinite variety of majority rule cycles may occur over alternative nonuniform apportioning probability distributions. For example, (.40, .20, .40) is majority preferred to (.35, .55, .10), which is majority preferred to (.20, .40, .40), which is majority preferred to (.10, .35, .55). In turn, (.10, .35, .55) is majority preferred to (.40, .20, .40), thereby completing the cycle.

All of the programs may be said to satisfy a very limited form of generality in that each person has at least *some* chance of securing the grant in every case. But the probability functions are not sufficiently uniform to remove the cycling problem. In this case, a generality rule that limits lottery formulas to those with an impersonal, or uniform, distribution narrows the domain of choice to a single option which clearly eliminates the majoritarian cycle.

Table 12.1 also indicates incentives that different individuals, parties, or regions may have in securing stochastically favorable treatment. Lobbying or other investments that can be used to shift policies from a uniform distribution to a privately favorable formula will clearly be forthcoming in cases in which favorable treatment can be secured. The second beneficiary would clearly have an incentive to expend resources to secure the first formula. The third would lobby for the fifth formula. A statistical generality rule eliminates incentives to lobby the legislature for privately favorable stochastic formulas by ruling out such possibilities.

B. Generality and social insurance

The problem of designing a social insurance program is in many respects similar to that of the random assignment problem just analyzed. Program benefits are granted on the basis of unknown random future events: unemployment, medical emergencies, foul weather, earthquakes, and other calamities. The probabilities of each of these events may differ significantly among the members of a country as a whole but may be very similar for individuals within a given occupation, region, or state. Therefore, selecting the basis for coverage, in effect, changes the probability function for awarding, here compensatory, grants. (Other aspects of coverage – the extent to which contingencies are insured and the manner of funding – generate political problems analogous to those already analyzed in the public service and taxation chapters.)

Any self-funded insurance program necessarily has ex post benefits that are more concentrated than permitted for a deterministic program constrained by the generality principle. Such programs might seem to be ruled out by the generality norm. But ex post differentiation is the nature of all true insurance programs, hence strict application of the generality principle might at first seem to imply that no social insurance programs qualify. But, as noted earlier, insurance programs may satisfy ex ante generality if the expected benefits from the insurance programs are uniformly distributed among the electorate. This constraint may rule out many current practices, but it does not rule out social insurance, per se. For example, the requirements of ex ante generality are clearly satisfied if each insured contingency is equally likely, and equally valued, by all within the polity of interest. In other cases, social insurance remains politically problematic for several reasons. First, much of our previous analysis of differences in probabilities, services, and tax prices is relevant. Cycling on any combination of these policy parameters may occur in legislative deliberating about the areas covered and manner of funding similar to those of deterministic programs already discussed. The possibility of differential treatment encourages those who expect particular benefits to form coalitions and to lobby in order to secure preferential treatment.

Second, the possibility of unequal treatment creates opportunities for changing the breadth and magnitude of coverage within a single insurance area. In some cases, the generality of an insurance program clearly increases as its inclusiveness increases. For example, it is clear that a nationwide natural catastrophe insurance program tends to be more general than national coverage of specific natural disasters such as earthquakes or floods. Both the benefits and probabilities of occurrence are often more uniform for broader programs than for narrow ones. On the other hand, increasing the breadth and magnitude of coverage are areas in which the distribution of benefits and costs may be substantially unequal. So long as the probability or magnitude of a particular catastrophe is not independent of the identity of those to be insured, incentives to include or exclude coverage of this or that catastrophic event become an arena for rent seeking and/or a possible cleaving issue for majority coalitions.

Third, mandating equal ex ante expected net benefits in *an actuarial sense* promotes equity but only reduces rather than eliminates incentives for interest groups to lobby to secure advantage. No objective special advantages may be allowed, but subjective ones remain. Policies that have the same actuarial benefits for every individual, would, in many cases, be sufficiently general that all the political benefits of generality can be secured. Indeed, it is probably the best that can be achieved in practice. On the other hand, it bears noting that measuring benefits is more problematic for stochastic programs than for deterministic programs because the degree of risk aversion varies across individuals. As a consequence, insurance programs that are actuarially identical across individuals may, nonetheless, yield different expected net benefits for more or less risk-averse individuals. More risk-averse individuals gain greater subjective benefits from insurance coverage than more risk-loving individuals. These differential, expected subjective advantages may motivate interest group activities and generate coalitional instability. Even in such cases, however, a restriction that all social insurance programs satisfy actuarial equality increases political efficiency insofar as it constrains the range of majoritarian cycles and reduces the intensity of rent seeking by constraining the range of alternative insurance programs that might be drafted.

C. State-sponsored contests

The preceding analysis has implicitly focused on settings in which individuals do not themselves directly control their own eligibility for program benefits. In such cases, the criteria for apportioning claims have no direct behavioral consequences. On the other hand, it is clear that only a few stochastically determined services completely satisfy this assumption. A person cannot control her age, but she can clearly affect the likelihood of requiring medical care, unemployment support, or fire protection through personal choices to invest in various forms of personal capital holdings or risk-reducing lifestyles. A completely general insurance program may escape the problem of adverse selection but not that of moral hazard.

Stochastic and nonstochastic programs directly affect incentives for private decision making in similar ways. Individuals are less inclined to purchase substitutes for publicly provided services and more inclined to purchase complements. Thus, public insurance programs reduce incentives for individuals to take steps to reduce personal risk and may be said to encourage complementary risk-taking behavior. In the case of insurance programs, these incentive effects are often inadvertent, but there are other programs that are, in effect, contests, which aim to narrowly reward or punish individuals for specific accomplishments. Are such programs consistent with the generality principle?

Such contests are not consistent with the generality principle in cases in which program benefits are conferred on the basis of criteria that are not uniform within the polity as a whole. A general lottery is permitted, but not a lottery in which free tickets are distributed to persons in a single region or subgroup of the polity. As previously noted, a general lottery is consistent with ex ante generality because anyone can purchase a ticket, and all tickets are equal before the drawing. But a biased contest that excludes some members of the polity from the game or gives significantly greater odds of winning to one or another subset of players violates the norm.

In cases in which contest rewards are conditioned on more elaborate forms of behavior than purchasing tickets, the more unusual the kind of behavior rewarded or punished, and the more narrow the distribution of the sanction, the less likely is generality satisfied. Here, behavioral criteria themselves are similar to any other discriminatory rule. A particular subgroup receives a service or punishment not equally available to all within the relevant public service area. Overtly discriminatory contests are ruled out by the generality principle. For example, policies that dictate the award of governmental contracts only to members of defined minority groups clearly violate any generality norm. As we have demonstrated in our earlier discussions, any discriminatory element creates a cleaving point for majority coalitions that tends to generate cycles, which, in turn, creates incentives for rent-seeking activity.

Discriminatory contests may be consistent with the generality principle if considered only as a means – and not as an end. In those cases in which the behavior rewarded is the production of public services, contests are simply one of the production methods or remuneration schemes that may be used. So long as discriminating contests are consistent with our discussion of issues concerned with public production (see Chapter 10), they may be used by a polity constrained by the generality principle. For example, national defense is a pure public good for all those within the boundaries protected. Medals and other recognition granted to outstanding service or heroism in the line of military duty is a compensation system that tends to reduce the cost of achieving higher levels of defense from given inputs by rewarding producers for superior performance.

Such reward systems may be locally general insofar as they are open to all those who might produce the service of interest and are granted on the basis of performance rather than on nonperformance aspects of personal identity. Stochastically rewarding a subset of especially effective producers of a public service in some cases may provide broad incentives for superior performance while it may reduce the cost of the "bonus" program over its equivalent deterministic counterpart.

D. Stochastic elements of crime and punishment

The enforcement arm of the criminal justice system operates as such a contest in reverse. Insofar as many criminals get off scot-free, the criminal justice system punishes only a subset of individuals who produce public bads – those who are caught and punished. In this sense, the imperfect enforcement of a general law is analogous to the contest examples discussed earlier. Here the contest punishes the production of public bads rather than rewards the production of a public good. So long as the probability of capture and conviction is independent of the identity of the criminal, ex ante, equality before the law exists and the requirements of generality are satisfied. The ex ante expected penalty for a given crime or sequence of crimes should be the same for all potential criminals. Crime is a "contest" in which the stochastic production of bads is discouraged by submitting crime producers to a somewhat random punishment.

The generality principle itself provides relatively little guidance about what activities should be punished, beyond allowing public nuisances to be sanctioned. Insofar as the behavior punished is universally held to be noxious, laws that curtail such behavior may be said to satisfy generality. However, the existence of any comparative advantage in activities that violates the laws of property, persons, or regulation necessarily implies that the financial/subjective burdens of such laws are not perfectly uniform. This is perhaps most obviously the case for various environmental and health regulations that impose most of the regulatory burden on a few firms or regions within a country, but it is no less true of traffic laws that increase revenues for companies that manufacture safety equipment while reducing sales of high performance cars and tires or property laws that differentially impact those with special skills at stealth or guile. The burden of securing reductions in noxious behavior – criminal law – naturally falls most heavily on those who have the most to gain from criminalized activities.

In cases in which the laws passed, or at least the process by which the laws were passed, may plausibly have been agreed to from behind a veil of ignorance – generality in the large may be said to be satisfied. For contractarians, the test of the Rawlsian veil circumscribes the range of behaviors that can legitimately be called crimes. In most cases, it may be argued that even those who remain committed to illegal activities secure net benefit from the laws that turn them into outlaws. For example, very skilled thieves may benefit if theft is illegal because property is more plentiful when the rules of contract and property are enforced. Illicit drug cartels and salesmen benefit from higher salaries and prices as law enforcement reduces competitive pressures. Minor inequities do not violate the generality principle insofar as the rules themselves are broad and confer more or less uniform benefits.

When a variety of alternative regulations are possible, we have argued that generality requires legislatures to minimize the concentration of the regulatory burden. We have not, in this volume, directly addressed the issue of what should be legal or illegal or what should be in the public or private domain. Rather, we have argued that whatever laws or other policies are legislated, they should be impersonal and have, at least, ex ante uniform consequences on those governed. This chapter has demonstrated that even services that are not uniform can be chosen in a manner that realize the political efficiency of the generality principle so long as ex ante generality for political decision makers obtains. The consequences of government policies may be unequal as long as they are general at the moment of the relevant political decision.

E. Conclusion: Statistical uniformity and constitutional choice

Our analysis of statistical uniformity indirectly complements and extends the contractarian analyses of Rawls (1971) and Buchanan and Tullock (1962) as well as the more utilitarian analysis of Harsanyi (1955) who all rely upon the principle of stochastic uniformity in their more fundamental philosophical enterprises. Generalized and uniform uncertainty in the former analyses reduces decision costs at the stylized constitutional convention. Generalized and uniform uncertainty in our analysis reduces decision-making cost in majoritarian democracy.[2] Insofar as politics are evenhanded, contractarians might argue that whatever legislation and enforcement of the law that emerges from a constitutional convention is general insofar as the agreed upon process of collectivization is tantamount to a lottery that generates uncertain benefits and uncertain costs. We have argued that procedures that violate generality in day-to-day legislation tend unnecessarily to increase the costs of governance by promoting rent seeking and reducing the stability of majority coalition governance.

In the end, whether the citizenry is willing to play the political game, the legitimacy of the government is a consequence of the distribution of decisions reached. We have argued that polities that adhere to the generality principle will be more consistent, less arbitrary, and less costly to run, in other words, more desirable than polities that do not.[3]

Social insurance and lotteries are methods of providing unequal services in special circumstances or locations without forsaking political efficiency. These institutions can provide the impartial equal treatment required by the generality principle and thereby preserve ex ante generality for the relevant decision makers. Political generality may be achieved in a variety of ways, most of which are consistent with notions of fairness, although the efficiency appeal of generality remains relevant even for those unconcerned with equity.[4]

13 Generality without uniformity: Federalism

In this chapter we demonstrate that in a federal system some programs that are ruled out by a generality constraint at one level of government may be permitted at another. A well-functioning federal structure of government can allow some departures from structure-wide uniformity while retaining the political efficiency advantage of adherence to the generality principle. Some services that fail to be sufficiently general at a more inclusive level of membership in political community may be acceptable at less inclusive levels of government or within smaller self-financing and autonomous service districts. A federalized structure of government can provide heterogeneous services while satisfying the strictures of generality.

The proponents of federal systems of governance have long touted the various efficiency-enhancing properties of decentralized political institutions. It has often been argued that federalism is a good solution to public service provision in cases in which ordinary economic efficiency requires nonuniform services across various regions of the country insofar as preferences, wealth, or circumstances vary significantly. Our generality defense of federalism is largely consistent with this conventional analysis, but it differs in approach and implication for assignment of tasks. Federalism allows generality to be adhered to at the level of every governmental body responsible for making collective program decisions while it allows departures from uniformity in the federation as a whole. Federalism allows political transactions costs to be minimized while realizing the advantages of locally heterogeneous service levels. In this sense, federal systems may be said to be a first-best institutional arrangement that produces outcomes that cannot be replicated even by an idealized democratic central government.

A. Homogeneity here does not require homogeneity there

Federalism is a hierarchical system of governance that divides responsibilities for various government activities among a nested series of political units, each with an assigned jurisdiction. The formal structure is often organized in "levels," in which the inclusive polity (the country) is divided into nonoverlapping activity or service areas (states), which are themselves subdivided into smaller areas (counties), which may themselves be subdivided into townships, and so forth. Taxing and spending decisions relevant to assigned activities are made separately by each subdivision of the inclusive territory. The central government is limited to making decisions relevant only to its own narrowly specified set of activities.

It is important to recognize that the generality principle can be applied at each level of government in such a way as to ensure that all persons within a particular service district receive the same level of service. Heterogeneous service levels may occur within the country as a whole even though each service district is bound by the generality principle. Adjacent districts may choose different service levels. Regional demands or supplies for public services vary, for example, as climate, population, population density, and wealth vary (Oates, 1972).

It is clear that such nonuniformity in service levels or combinations among regions within a country as a whole would violate the generality principle if the programs should be administered by a single unified government. The political efficiency of a unified state would suffer as various subregions of the country conspired to receive superior services funded by other regions of the country. Regional lobbying groups would similarly invest resources in conflict over who would receive the greater benefit or bear the lowest cost for services provided. Regional discrimination entails high political costs in a unitary state.

A federal government that is itself constrained by the generality principle and that clearly has demarcated fiscal authority avoids the political problems of heterogeneous service levels because every collective choice may be made by a governing body that is constrained by its own applicable generality principle. The end results, therefore, parallel those analyzed previously. Production, distribution, and funding of local government services in each jurisdiction would conform to generality by following the mandates outlined in Chapter 10. Local services would be provided uniformly within each service district, produced in a diffuse manner to ensure local relative price neutrality, and financed with a broad-based tax on those within the area of interest. Any project desired by a subset of the polity that fails the generality test at the one level of government may attempt it again at a lower level. If it fails at national, state, or local levels, the service may be produced in a special service district composed of interested parties. Insofar as the special service district has the power to tax, it differs from a private club and would be constrained by the generality principle.

The discussion to this point has ignored several complications. As noted, there may exist potentially productive goods and services that involve genuine publicness, in the classic Samuelsonian sense, with beneficiary ranges that do not extend over the full membership or territory of the inclusive central polity. As previously suggested, a federal political structure would allow these services to be financed–provided by units of government that are more closely correspondent with ranges of benefit and, hence, demand. But the persons who are direct benefeciaries may, themselves, prefer that the activities be financed by the central government because, in this way, they can effectively secure differential gains at the expense of others in the inclusive polity who are not primary beneficiaries but who will be subjected to taxes (Hoyt and Toma, 1989; Congleton, 1994).

An example may be helpful. Suppose that flood protection qualifies under genuine publicness criteria; collective financing–provision promises to yield net benefits. But the direct or primary beneficiaries are persons who locate in potential flood plains; persons in the highlands secure no benefits at all, at least not directly. A federalized structure of governance might allow some appropriately defined regional authority to levy general taxes on those who are potential direct beneficiaries with revenues devoted to the financing of flood protection, which would then be generally available to all persons within the scope of the authority.

These direct beneficiaries might recognize, however, that their own positions possibly could be enhanced by a shift of flood protection services to the central government. In this way, the expected benefits of flood protection might be secured, but at a lower tax cost. Nonbeneficiaries who locate in the highlands might be forced to finance some part of the benefits enjoyed exclusively by those who locate in the potential flood plain.

Even in the absence of an operative generality constraint at the central government level, however, potential beneficiaries of a localized public good or service, like flood protection, must also recognize that central government financing of differentially beneficial programs is unlikely to emerge piecemeal or one at a time. Even with no generality constraint, localized programs that promise differential benefits to specific subgroups of citizenry must be somehow packaged in a set that will command majority approval. Recognition by the flood protection beneficiaries (or their lobby) that in order to secure central government financing they may be required to package their program with others for, say, harbor dredging, forest fire prevention, and urban transit (some or all of which may or may not exhibit genuine publicness qualities sufficient to warrant collective financing) should temper pressures that favor centralization as opposed to federalism.

Under a fully operative generality constraint, the central government would not be able to finance or provide differentially beneficial goods and services, even if these could not be provided efficiently by nongovernmental or market organizations. This constraint would effectively force political organization, or reorganization, toward federalized structures and might involve not only devolution of some centrally financed activities to existing state units but, also, the establishment of other political units such as regional authorities, special districts, and so on.

B. Generality and mobility

Tiebout-type mobility (Tiebout, 1956) among separate jurisdictions increases the appeal of the generality principle while reinforcing its stability. Adherence to the generality principle implies that all persons within a particular unit have available (or at least expect) the same level of all services. Tiebout-type mobility implies that any individual who prefers a fiscal package in some other jurisdiction could simply migrate to that community. Individuals are thereby sorted by demands for public services so that all residents within a locality will prefer, as well as receive, the same level of all services. Our previous analysis indicates that the efficiency gains of adherence to a generality principle are most uniform and certain in such settings.

Tiebout-type adjustment also implies that competitive pressures ensure that local public services are produced at the same minimal cost. Any community that can provide a bundle of services at a lower cost than other communities attracts residents, at least at the margins of adjustment, from those high-cost communities because the same services are available at a lower tax price. In the limit, communities are completely stratified by demand for local services, and all local services are produced at least cost; tax prices tend to equal the marginal cost of providing services to community members.[1]

It bears noting that the classic Tiebout-type efficiency results have always been based upon the assumption that local governments provide uniform service levels to all within the bounds of every local jurisdiction. If local governments are free to discriminate in tax price or service level, local governments could reduce mobility by treating those who exit differently from those who remain behind. (Emigrants might be targets of very high last-period taxes or a substantial exit charge.) If local ruling coalitions are stable, the reduced mobility made possible by internal fiscal discrimination yields a series of independent fiscal fiefdoms. The fiscal dividend secured by reducing mobility can be used to provide differential benefits for members of the ruling coalition. In cases in which ruling coalitions are unstable, as previously analyzed, both local fiscal packages and population levels would be unstable as majoritarian cycles occur through time. Tiebout-type mobility and competition under a generality principle not only assure that services are uniformly provided in every community but that production satisfies the local demands for government services.

C. Federalism and the origins of uniform service levels

Although much of the popular intuitive appeal of the generality principle is based on cultural norms of fairness, our analysis has focused on political-efficiency gains implied by alternative structures and means of governance. We have argued that, from behind a veil of ignorance, all persons would prefer institutions that ensure general treatment to those that allow significant discriminatory discretion on the part of the political authorities. The political efficiency associated with the generality principle arises because of effects of general service provision on incentives for political action. Federalized institutions can provide the impartial equal treatment required by the generality principle and thereby preserve ex ante generality for the relevant decision makers. The generality principle will have broad support at a hypothetical Rawlsian convention in a wide variety of circumstances. Such hypothetical conventions provide a thought laboratory in which alternative institutional arrangements can be evaluated by using contractarian normative propositions in much the same manner that the conventional Pareto criterion allows a similarly abstract analysis of policy alternatives.

Mobility among alternative communities in a real federation allows many of the propositions of the hypothesized constitutional convention to be tested in an ongoing real social setting insofar as citizenship in a local community is a matter of choice rather than birth. Tiebout-type mobility is often characterized as voting with one's feet. Here, location reveals that one prefers the services, amenities, and job prospects associated with one location over all others – net of moving costs. The smaller are these moving costs, or threshold costs generally, and the smaller are the variations in other nongovernmental services, the more location itself can be interpreted to imply consent.

To the extent that the generality principle increases political efficiency and thereby yields a relatively attractive fiscal package, the generalization dimension itself becomes one along which communities will compete, one with another. Communities that operate in accordance with a generality principle will attract individuals who fear arbitrary treatment in an unrestrained community and/or who prefer stable levels of service over time.

The success of such local communities would in the end cause fiscally similar communities to adopt similar restrictions. Thus, a positive implication of our analysis is that local governments should be observed widely to provide substantially uniform service packages to all their citizens. As in other domains of competition, a pattern of providing uniform services within a service district need not be a self-conscious decision. Only governments that provide uniform services survive in the long-term competition for residents.

In this manner, federalism is a vehicle by which a significant fraction of local governmental services – or at least pivotal services such as education, transport, and police protection – come to be provided in accordance with the generality principle in the long run.[2] Moreover, the sorting process that leads to more or less uniform demands for local services also implies that the generality principle will be a more stable rule in a setting of competitive local governments than it tends to be in the less competitive environment of national government. These implications may be a partial explanation for the widespread use of common property amenities to attract residents to towns, villages, and private condominium communities, in spite of the well-known commons problems associated with communal amenities.

As the appeal of generality is realized at local levels, one would expect to find local governments lobbying for similar restrictions to be placed on higher levels of governments. Generality at higher levels reduces conflict among local governments for special treatment and increases the coalitional stability making it easier for local governments to plan. Indirectly, therefore, federalism may be one of the factors that explains the existence of significant generality at higher level governments as well.

D. Conclusion: Federalism as the principal vehicle for targeting services

Nonuniformity is not a political issue in cases in which uniformity is a technological consequence of production, as in national defense or environmental regulation of freely dispersing effluents. In areas in which government policies are not technologically constrained to have uniform consequences, we have argued that policy alternatives generally should be constrained to have uniform consequences as a means of promoting political efficiency. However, as noted in Chapter 12, completely uniform consequences are not required to achieve the increased political efficiency associated with the generality principle. The political advantage of the generality principle requires uniformity only within the policy and service areas under the control of the relevant political decision-making body, and uniformity only in the ex ante sense that all politically active parties expect the same consequence from the policy under consideration.

In a federal state constrained by the generality principle, policies continue to have uniform consequences on individuals who live within the same service jurisdiction. Each person within a jurisdiction has available the same services, although service levels may vary across districts. Federalism allows heterogeneous results but preserves the political efficiencies generated by the generality principle insofar as each policymaking body is constrained at the moment of choice. Multiple levels of independent political decision making allow the possibility of heterogeneous service levels among many different service districts, each one of which is constrained by the generality principle.

This and the preceding chapter have demonstrated that even services that are not uniform can be chosen in a manner that realizes political efficiency so long as ex ante generality for political decision makers obtains. The consequences of government policies may be unequal so long as they are general at the moment of the relevant political decision. Federalism, social insurance, and lotteries are methods of providing unequal services in special circumstances or locations without forsaking political efficiency.

We have not, in this chapter or elsewhere in this volume, addressed in depth the issue of what should be legal or illegal or what should be in the public or private domain. Rather, we have argued that whatever laws or other policies are legislated should be impersonal. Insofar as politics are evenhanded, the legislation and enforcement of the law is tantamount to a lottery that generates uncertain benefits and uncertain costs. In the end, whether the electorate is willing to play the game – the public legitimacy of the government – is a consequence of the distribution of decisions reached. We have argued that polities that adhere to the generality principle will be more consistent, less arbitrary, and less costly to run than polities that do not.[3]

We acknowledge that any service that is equally provided in some sense, will be unequal in another, so long as people and circumstances differ. Uniform provision of governmental service levels implies different benefit levels unless all users are homogeneous. To the extent that voting and/or lobbying are based upon subjective benefits, it is subjective benefits that have to be the root of the analysis of politics. On the other hand, to the extent that benefits have measurable correlates, such as monetary net advantage or objective service levels, generality is discernible and remedial. More generality is clearly distinguishable from less generality in such cases.

Federalism clearly allows uniform services to be a consequence of competition rather than a manipulated feature of constitutional design. In this, federalism is perhaps the best real laboratory of the appeal of the generality principle. While it is clear that local departures are commonplace, the broad outlines of policies in local governments – their uniform provision of all major services, the proportional tax systems (largely on property), and restrictions on the use of debt to finance public service – are largely consistent with the generality principle, as examined in this book. To this extent, at least, federalism may be said to prove the case for politics by principle.

It may also be said that our analysis of the generality principle makes the first-best case for federalism. Federalism is often claimed to be a second-best form of government insofar as a central government could, in principle, implement the results of an ideal competitive result while avoiding the costs of maintaining many decision-making bodies and/or reducing moving costs induced by bad local government. Our analysis makes it clear that a central government that is broadly majoritarian in its operation cannot provide differential heterogeneous program benefits without incurring significant political decision costs. Rent seeking and coalitional instability are direct implications of the potential ability of the central government to discriminate among regions, peoples, or income groups. Moreover, there is no obvious reason for efficient policies to be sustained in an unconstrained majoritarian setting. A federal system constrained by the generality principle avoids these political decision costs while providing a vehicle for locally efficient production.

PART FOUR
Prospect

14   The political shape
of constitutional order

In this final chapter, we return to the abstracted arguments developed in the first part of the book. The several applications examined in Chapters 6 through 13 of the text should have been sufficient to demonstrate the normative relevance of the generality principle in the turn-of-the-century politics that we now experience. Policy arguments in support of free, open, and nondiscriminatory trade; flatter and more uniform taxation; nonparticularized standards for environmental regulation and public goods provision; devolution of political authority to more adequately defined areas of special benefits and against means testing for transfers – indeed, against discriminatory treatment of any sort – these arguments find common philosophical grounding in the rule or norm for political generality.

There is a categorical distinction to be drawn between arguments for depoliticization, per se, and the application of the generality principle over those sectors of interaction that are politicized, although there are relationships that stem from feedbacks between prospects for discriminatory exploitation and the range of politicization itself, some of which will be discussed later in this chapter.

Specifically, this book is about the constitutional structure of those sectors of social interaction that are politicized; it is not directly about drawing some borderline between these (public) sectors and the private (market) sectors. We recognize, of course, that arguments in support of many of the same policy thrusts noted (e.g., free trade and nondiscriminatory taxation) may be derived from the classical liberal precept of minimal coercion, or its obverse, maximal individual liberty from collective intrusion. This second normative impulse has been much more central in modern discourse than the normative inferences from generalization that we have stressed here. By implication, if not directly, most classical liberals have seemed willing to trade off equality or nondiscrimination in political treatment in exchange for apparent shrinkages in some measured size of the politicized sectors. F. A. Hayek is, of course, the major exception to this stance, and his monumental treatise, *The Constitution of Liberty* (1960), developed generality as its dominating normative theme.

Our effort in this book is aimed to fall squarely within this Hayekian realm of discourse. Our emphasis, both in analysis and application, is on the desirability of avoiding (or reducing) the discriminatory politics that must describe what we may call the natural logic of majoritarian democracy.

In Sections A and B, we examine the relationships between generality in politics and the extension of politics by postulating, in turn, models within which the two features diverge dramatically from agreed upon classical liberal norms but in differing directions. In Section A, we look briefly at a setting in which, overall, the extension of politics is kept within bounds, but in which there is no attempted adherence, either explicitly or implicitly, to a generality norm. Then, in Section B, we analyze the converse case – a setting in which the generality norm is strictly observed, both in idea and in practice, but in which politics is extended without limit other than that imposed by the will of majority coalitions.

It is not surprising that the choice between these models, if any such inclusive and pairwise systemic selection should ever be confronted, would involve a trade-off, of sorts, between political efficiency and economic efficiency. More specifically, allocative distortions would arise in both models, but from quite different sources and subject to quite different measures for waste of value. In the model in Section A – that of the small but discriminatory state – resource wastage emerges in large part because of majoritarian rent seeking, reflected in efforts made by persons to secure membership in majority coalitions – membership that would, in its turn, promise opportunities to gain from discrimination against nonmajority members. By comparison, in the model in Section B – that of the large but generalized public sector – excess burdens of the sort familiar to economists would be relatively large because of the incentive effects operative on both sides of the account. The trade-off between rent seeking and excess burden inefficiencies is explicitly discussed in Section C.

There is also the more direct and perhaps more important trade-off between perceived fairness on the one hand and overt discrimination on the other – a trade-off that assumes relevance only when and if politics is modeled differently under different circumstances. The relationship between alternative models of politics and the generality norm is discussed in Section D.

Finally, in Section E, we make an effort to bring the discussion down from the lofty rafters of political philosophy to issues of practical relevance for political–constitutional reform at the end of the century. How can the welfare state be contained while democratic decision procedures remain in place? And what are the predicted consequences of explicit departures from the generality norm?

A. Minimal, but discriminatory, majoritarian democracy

In this section, we examine, in brief, the workings of a polity that is narrowly restricted in size relative to the aggregate economy but that remains open to the natural processes of majoritarian democracy within these size limits. Imagine a setting described by the presence of an effectively enforceable constitutional limit on the aggregate size of the politicized sector, say, a limit of one-quarter of gross product value, as measured by GDP – a limit well below that observed in modern Western nations. Assume, however, that this restriction is the only operative constitutional constraint, other than those that are postulated to describe majoritarian democracy itself (open franchise, periodic elections, free entry into political activity, and so on). Specifically, we assume that there are no restrictions on discrimination among and between members of separate political coalitions.

As the analysis of earlier chapters demonstrated, in this stylized setting, all positions on the diagonal (used here as a metaphor for positions that meet the generality criterion) will be majority dominated. Regardless of the composition of the majoritarian coalition, no nondiscriminatory alternatives will remain in the political choice set. And, as the earlier analysis also showed, all relevant alternatives will incorporate distributional elements, possibly on both sides of the political account.

Some goods that are generally beneficial to all members of the inclusive polity may be provided collectively, but only to the extent that the members of the ruling coalition value their own shares more highly than direct fiscal transfers. In any case, it is evident that the budgetary mix under the political structure postulated here would be heavily weighted toward transfers and away from the financing of commonly valued public goods and services. And as the political decision authority rotates among separately organized majority coalitions, we should predict continually shifting compositions of persons as between net taxpayer and net recipient groups.

The standard excess burdens of positive and negative taxes will be present, and there will be efficiency losses generated by the induced behavioral changes on both sides of the fiscal account. These standard excess burdens will, however, be quite limited in this model because we have assumed that the aggregate size of the public sector remains small relative to the whole economy.

This familiar source of inefficiency is likely to be swamped in effect by a second source, summarized under the rent seeking rubric, which emerges to make the whole structure of discriminatory politics politically inefficient. To the extent that membership in the decisive majority coalition is tied directly to prospects for securing valued payoffs, either through receipt of monetary transfer payments or through exemption–exclusion from taxation levied to finance both transfers and public goods, individuals will find it personally profitable to invest resources in efforts to join, as well as to organize, potential majority coalitions.

As the formal analysis in social choice theory demonstrates, there can be no majority equilibrium when the choice alternatives embody units of value that are partitionable among persons. Majority voting rules must, in these settings, exhibit the familiar and much-discussed cycling among the alternative solutions, and electoral replacement of any dominant coalition by another requires only the presentation of one of the many other nondominated majoritarian imputations. (Recall the models in Chapter 3.) It is this ever-present prospect for increasing one's personal payoff in a newly formed coalition that prompts persons to invest in "politics" as such – investment that is, in a meaningful sense, "wasteful."

It might be suggested that the constitutional structure of the limited-government model considered here would embody criteria for fairness that ensures, at least probabilistically, that participants retain equal chances to become members of majority coalitions, thereby ensuring equal eligibility for receipt of transfer payments (and, conversely, equal prospects of being members of the minority subjected to discriminatory taxation). Such results might be generated, however, by any of many relatively costless methods of rotation among the distributional alternatives, the use of any one of which could eliminate the destruction of economic value measured roughly by total rent-seeking outlay.

B. Maximal, but nondiscriminatory, majoritarian democracy

We propose, now, to examine the possible workings of majoritarian democracy in a constitutional setting in which a generality constraint is effectively enforced, but in which there are no limits on the aggregate share of the economy that is politicized.

In our matrix metaphor of earlier chapters, the model now restricts the alternatives of majoritarian choice to positions that lie along the n-dimensional diagonal, but it places no restrictions on the range or extent of politicization. In particular, there is no presumption that the public sector is limited to the finance–production–provision of public goods, defined in the Samuelsonian sense of nonrivalry (nonpartitionability) and nonexcludability. As demonstrated earlier, for all such goods, generality is technologically guaranteed for one side of the account. But political organization of fully partitionable, and potentially excludable, goods and services as well as direct *transfers* may also be observed. The constitutive requirement here is that if such nonpublic goods are collectively provided, all participants must be offered equal quantities (e.g., government must supply all families with milk if any one family is so provided, and, more importantly, a direct transfer of a dollar to one family must be matched by a dollar transfer to every family).

We must first specify more carefully what tax-share distribution will qualify under the postulated constitutional norm for generality. As discussed in Chapter 5, we define generality in terms of input supply, and, more particularly, as analyzed in Chapter 6, we interpret the tax-share norm to be one that levies equal rates of tax on each unit of income received. That is to say, a flat-rate or proportional tax on all income, with no exclusions, exemptions, deductions, or credits is dictated.

As discussed in Chapter 11, we should predict that the aggregate size of the collective sector would be large relative to the total economy and that direct transfers, in the form of demogrants, would make up a large part of the budget. In the aggregate, however, allocative inefficiency would not be of the magnitude conventionally associated with comparably large public outlay. There are two reasons for this conclusion. As noted, because of the generality requirement, persons would not find it advantageous to initiate resource-wasting investment in seeking differentially favored nongeneral spending programs and/or special tax treatment. A second reason for limitation on potential efficiency loss stems from the effects of generality itself on nonpolitical behavior. The magnitude of excess burdens, both those of taxes and transfers, is related to the elasticities of behavioral responses; that is, to the substitutability among alternative behavioral options. To the extent that an operative generality constraint closes off options, there is necessarily a limit to potential response. If *all* incomes are subjected to a single flat-rate tax, there is no burden that arises as a result of persons shifting activity among various income sources.

Excess burdens may remain large, however, in the extended transfer state that would describe this model. The generality norm would necessarily exclude both leisure and shadow economic activity from the tax base. Persons would clearly produce less economic value than might be generated under a more restricted, but still general, politicized regime.

C. Generality within some limits; politics bound but loosely

In the institutional reality that is observed in Western democracies, neither of the models sketched out in the two preceding sections is descriptively accurate. What we observe is a mixture of both models, with additional elements that both disturb and satisfy the classical liberal who prefers both limited government and adherence to the generality principle in its operation. As they operate in modern practice, governments command an ever-increasing share of economic value – a share that increased dramatically over the course of the twentieth century, and one that, perhaps surprisingly, shows no sign of decreasing even in the postsocialist period. And, predictably, the redistributive or transfer component of the politicized sector has increased disproportionately, especially during the last half of the century. At the same time, however, the excesses that might be predicted from the very logic of majoritarianism do not seem to have emerged. We seem to remain at some distance from de Jasay's (1985) "churning state," even if explicit adherence to a generality norm is nowhere to be found.

What we observe is, instead, a very loose and quite selective generality principle in operation – one that does serve to keep democratic discrimination within some limits, but without any overt recognition of principled constraints. Nor does the politics of modern democracy embody nondiscrimination even as a central normative thrust. Indeed, the opposing principle is more descriptive; politics is deliberately discriminatory. It is, however, discriminatory only along specific dimensions of constituency identity. Discrimination on the basis of direct political affiliation, gender, race, ethnicity, or religion is, by commonly shared precepts as well as legal rules, out of bounds. (An exception here is provided in the United States through its affirmative action initiatives, which counter widely shared value standards. Indeed, reaction to these initiatives measures, in some part, the strength of the nondiscrimination precept.) In dramatic contrast, politically directed discrimination by age, economic status, occupational or professional category, personal behavioral habits, geographical location, and many other defining characteristics is deemed wholly legitimate. And, of course, intersecting coalitions defined by such criteria can accomplish much of what a more specific politically motivated discrimination might address. Modern politics does seem to be partially driven "by interest" rather than "by principle," to put the reverse thrust on this book's main title, although some principles of nondiscrimination carry over from the rule of law, and these operate independently to limit, to a degree, the natural politics of majority rule.

There is a danger that the pressures exerted by growth in the relative size of the politicized sector – pressures that erupt in public reaction to high and increasing tax rates and measured by behavioral responses that generate excess burdens of the orthodox variety – will prompt further movement away from generality, notably in the transfer sector of budgets. As we have emphasized, the introduction of means testing will increase rent seeking or political inefficiency as it promises to reduce, somewhat, conventional excess burdens. Classical liberals, especially, should beware of following a false god. *How* politics impacts on the citizenry is as important as *how much*. Of particular concern is the apparent political viability of targeted programs of tax preference on the one side and differential spending programs on the other, as opposed to across-the-board changes, either in taxes or in spending. To the extent that such targeting goes on, generality is, of course, violated.

D. Generality in noncontractarian visions of political order

To this point and throughout the analysis of the book, we have discussed the generality principle as if both its meaning and its presence or absence can be readily agreed to by detached observers (Adam Smith's, 1937/1776, impartial spectator). Such a presumption need not raise an objection, at least at the level of conceptual analysis rather than practical application, if some ultimate contractarian interpretation informs normative understanding of the whole political enterprise. And, as we noted in the introductory chapter, our effort proceeds from just such a philosophical base. At this point, we should recognize, however, that differing evaluative standards for political activity, and the place of individuals within it, might emerge from alternative normative foundations.

There are two distinct conceptualizations that warrant consideration. The first embodies a vision of society as a natural hierarchy in which some persons are "natural slaves" while others are "natural masters" or rulers. In any of the many variants of this conception, any principle of generality applicable over all members of the polity is misplaced. Clearly, differing rules apply to differing classes of persons. A second vision or conceptualization does not interpret the state or political order as a cooperative enterprise among separate individuals at all, whether these be equals or members of classes. Instead, society, or rather the collective, is prior to the individual, who exists normatively only in furtherance of the organic purpose of the collective itself. Generality in treatment among persons simply has no meaning in this vision.

As we indicated in Chapter 1, we shall not discuss these alternative visions of social and political order. They are introduced in this final chapter only to suggest that the normative appeal of generality becomes quite different to the extent that either or both of these visions enter into evaluation. In the hierarchical vision of social interaction, criteria of fairness may still be introduced to apply *within* class-defined categories of persons. Persons who classify themselves as members of the elite will claim some generality in treatment as among themselves, and they may, also, seek to promote norms of equal, even if subsidiary, treatment among the subjects.

By contrast, as noted, in the genuinely "organicist" vision of society, there may be little or no normative thrust toward any criterion of generality. Persons exist to fulfill roles or niches in the larger social unit, and persons do not exert legitimate normative claims to rights, entitlements, or status that might prompt interpersonal comparisons, one with another.

Little more than notice of these alternative visions of sociopolitical order is needed to suggest the intuitive appeal of the individualistic–contractarian vision upon which our whole emphasis is placed, in this book as well as in earlier writings. Relatively few citizens in modern democracies think much, if at all, about the philosophical foundations of the society in which they live. Their attitudes are, nonetheless, informed by an understanding that we may label as *democratic*, by which we refer to claims to be equal participants in social order, at least at some ultimate level of interaction.

E. Political economy in the twenty-first century

Competing visions of political order will continue to describe the philosophical dialogue, and the alternative visions will influence public attitudes toward politics, government, and the state. The noncontractarian visions, those described as hierarchical or organic, will likely survive despite their basic inconsistency with democracy in any meaningful interpretation. Neither of these models involves attribution of a central value to individual equality, in law, in politics, or more generally.

The contractarian perspective, in which individuals are necessarily equal in their potential capacities as responsible creators of their own values as well as choosers of their own actions, must somehow coexist with ideas that sublimate the interests of some persons to the dictates of others. These noncontractarian ideas are necessarily subversive to liberal democracy as a cooperative enterprise, and they tend to be reinforced by the natural logic of majority rule that operates by the creation–formation of categorical distinctions between those who are ruled and those who are rulers.

We might have expected, perhaps naively, that the bankruptcy of Marxist–socialist ideology, as revealed in the great 1989–91 revolutions, would have reinvigorated the contractarian ideals of an open and limited political order as complementary with an economy organized on market principles, and without intrusive politicization.[1] But we have not, at least by 1997, observed any postrevolutionary reduction in the zeal of the *dirigistes*, who seem, genuinely, to consider themselves both epistemologically and morally superior to their fellow citizens. With the Marxists, there was at least the pretense of scientific legitimization in the laws of historical development. With the post-Marxist *dirigistes*, there is nothing other than the raw and critically exposed claim that "the good" is revealed only to those who demand submission to their will. The exercise of such authority requires, of course, that persons as subjects be discriminatorily and differentially treated, as determined by the wisdom of the human gods. Nondiscrimination or generality in treatment would counter the putative thrust toward the good and the true, as discovered and revealed.

Political legitimacy must be earned, either by the persuasive force of an ideology, by exemplary leadership, or, finally, by some sense of community in which persons are treated separately but equally in their capacities as sharers in both the burdens and benefits of collective endeavor. The vulnerability of any political order that rests on acceptance of a noncontractarian, nonindividualist, nonconstitutionalist vision seems apparent, and any such order offers little promise in the new century. If this conclusion is accepted, directionally appropriate reform must aim toward rather then away from generality. The observed thrust of modern politics toward discrimination, toward targeted special treatment, must, at the least, be halted and ultimately reversed.

Western welfare states are overextended; this diagnosis is almost universally accepted. The fiscal crises, defined in part by public withdrawal of support, must not be met by further discrimination, by some trading off of the illusory gains of lowered fiscal burdens against some increase in targeting, whether through increased tax loopholes or benefits means testing. Such a path toward alleged "reform" can only reduce rather than increase the minimal sense of community, without which any political order incorporating individual liberty cannot long survive.

Endnotes

Chapter 1: Generality, law, and politics

1. Jules Coleman (1985) has extensively discussed the importance of the distinction between the criterial and the epistemological uses of agreement. In the latter, for example, in the operation of a jury, agreement is a means of discovering that which exists quite independently of the process itself.

2. The political and public reaction to the apparent violation of the generality precept embodied in specific legal and institutional discrimination, summarized under "affirmative action," demonstrates the importance of the precept in public legal understanding.

3. See Leoni (1961) for a general analysis of the self-organizing properties of a decentralized legal order that is built on *stare decisis*.

Chapter 2: Majoritarian democracy

1. Arrow (1951) is quite specific. He stated the following:

The objects of choice are social states. The most precise definition of a social state would be a complete description of the amount of each type of commodity in the hands of each individual, the amount of each productive resource invested in each type of productive activity, and the amounts of various types of collective activity. . . . (p. 17)

Sen (1970) was more succinct,

Each social state being a complete description of society, including every individual's position in it. (p. 152)

2. Consider a simple distributional game with three units of partitionable value. The imputation $(1, 1, 1)$ will not be in the set of alternatives among which shifting majority coalitions may select. This $(1, 1, 1)$ imputation is dominated for *any* majority by one of the set $(2, 0, 1)$, $(1, 0, 2)$, $(0, 2, 1)$, $(0, 1, 2)$, $(2, 1, 0)$, $(1, 2, 0)$. For other, and more general, examples, see the discussion in Chapter 3, and for further treatment, see Buchanan (1997).

Chapter 3: Eliminating the off-diagonals

1. See Congleton and Tollison (1996). The seminal paper in rent seeking is by Gordon Tullock (1967). For extension and application to the majoritarian setting, see Buchanan (1995b). And for a summary of the whole research program, see Tollison (1997).

2. Consider the familiar model in which three voters evaluate two genuinely public goods (e.g., college roommates deciding on the thermostat setting and lights-out time), as illustrated in Figure 3.6. Majority voting generates cycling over wide areas of surface, but the symmetry imposed by requiring that all solutions lie along any arbitrary line, L, converts the setting into one dimension and produces stability at the median preference position.

155

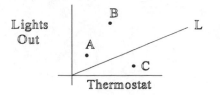

Figure 3.6. Three persons, two public goods.

3. We should note, however, that when preferences are single peaked, the profitability of majoritarian rent seeking is less than in settings in which single peakedness is absent. In the latter case, an alternative majority coalition may be organized by a shift in the multidimensional issue space. In the first case, by contrast, the median preference can be displaced only by "jumping over" (through bribes or other schemes) middle ranges along a single dimension.

Chapter 6: Generality and externality

1. More durable arrangements might call forth greater rent seeking at the preconstitutional level. However, the same uncertainty associated with the consequences of durable arrangements that makes agreement possible reduces the expected value of those arrangements to prospective rent seekers. Consequently, fewer resources are invested in the constitutional rent-seeking game than would have been invested in the ongoing game.

2. Of course such permanant assignments of use rights may be more or less general–rights of ownership, contract, and tort that are not restricted by bloodlines, class, religion, or race. Such unrestricted rights of ownership are common in modern Western countries, although they have not always been so. The generality of modern ownership rights doubtless contributes to their legitimacy of property law and both directly and indirectly to that of the government insofar as it is called on to intercede in a smaller, less controversial subset of policy areas.

3. Rights of ownership, contract, and tort that are not restricted by bloodlines, class, religion, or race are examples of a generality principle in law. Such unrestricted rights of ownership are common in modern Western countries. The generality of ownership rights doubtless contributes to their legitimacy and also to that of the polity insofar as it is called on to intercede in a smaller, less controversial subset of policy areas. (See Buchanan, Tollison, and Tullock, eds., 1980; Tollison and Congleton, eds., 1995.)

4. Note that the result here is the converse of the Paretian-liberal paradox discussed and analyzed by Amartya Sen (1970). In the Sen model, independent adjustment along each personal dimension generates a Nash equilibrium that is Pareto dominated. By contrast, in the model here, uniform adjustment (generality) may produce outcomes that are Pareto dominated by the Nash equilibrium itself.

5. In the case in which individuals are approximately risk neutral, we can continue to interpret the payoffs as outputs rather than utilities, as we have done throughout most of this volume. In this case, utility is linear in payoffs, and expected utility is proportional to expected payoffs.

Chapter 7: Market restriction and the generality norm

1. Extreme examples of rent seeking losses are characterized in Magee, Brock, and Young (1989). See also Krueger (1974) and Bhagwati (1982).

Chapter 8: The political efficiency of general taxation

1. The essential argument developed in this chapter was initially presented in James M. Buchanan (1993b).

2. For extended treatment of this approach to tax share distribution, see James M. Buchanan (1976).

3. We shall not discuss here an alternative construction that was introduced by Brennan and Buchanan (1980) in *The Power to Tax*. In that construction, government was modeled as a revenue-maximizing Leviathan, in which case the implications for the fiscal constitution are, of course, quite different from those that might be derived from either of the conventional approaches or from the model of majoritarian politics introduced in this book.

4. Lee and Snow (1993) criticized conventional tax analysis for its neglect of political incentives, but they did not explicitly develop a model of political process.

5. Objections may be raised to the argument that majority politics must embody discrimination. Why would it not be possible for members of a majority coalition to behave nondiscriminatorily? If, however, politicians tried to behave in this fashion, they would surely lose out in electoral contests with others who would promise to secure differential benefits for another coalition. The political leader who genuinely tries to promote the overall or general interest simply does not survive in democratic electoral politics. For further analysis, see Buchanan (1993a).

6. In the absence of single peakedness, there is no majority equilibrium, even with consideration limited to symmetric or general treatment alternatives. In the example here, nonpeakedness would appear bizarre because this feature would require that one person rank a medium tax rate lower than both a high rate and a low rate.

7. Exceptions would occur if a person considers the budgetary outlay to become productive only beyond certain limits. The financing of the Vietnam war offers a possible example. Many persons might have preferred either a lower or higher outlay to the moderate level actually carried out.

8. Becker (1983) has argued that the politics of competing interest groups will tend to generate a distribution of taxation that corresponds to that which will be optimal in the stylized model of the welfare economist. Becker's construction does not distinguish between majority and minority influences on outcomes. His analysis does not incorporate the workings of majoritarianism, as such.

9. This conclusion does not, of course, imply that there are no negative economic effects of capital gains taxation. The overall rate of economic growth may well be higher in a fiscal regime that exempts or favors capital gains. Our focus here is, however, on the applicability of the generality principle.

It may also be worth noting that the argument for favorable treatment of capital gains is much stronger under a tax rate structure that already involves differential rates than under a tax structure that applies the same rate to all sources.

10. Hartmut Kliemt (1995) made essentially the same argument advanced in this chapter in a more general discussion of the rule of law.

Chapter 10: Generality and the supply of government services

1. It bears noting in passing that not all goods with these properties are produced by governments. For example, broadcast radio and television programming are privately provided to all in the United States who live within a moderate distance of a broadcast tower without exclusion

and at no cost beyond purchase of a radio or television set. All within the service area receive the service provided. This manner of production, pricing, and dissemination is partly a result of licensing provisions and partly a result of the history of the technology of transmitting signals.

Moreover, exclusion technologies change through time as technological innovation takes place. It is now easy to exclude persons from broadcast programming, for example, by encoding the programs and controlling the supply of decoders, as can be done by renting decoders to subscribers. Such exclusion devices are used to finance the provision of many private services in which the nonrivalry in consumption and economies of scale in production extend to even broader audiences than local broadcasting does (e.g., satellite broadcast television and cellular telephone networks). Many government services are similarly more excludable today than they were at their inception.

2. Insofar as a proportional tax has been used to finance the service, and the demand for this service exhibits unit income elasticity, the fiscal setting would approximate decisions under a benefit tax when the service is provided to all, but this feature is not essential for the present discussion. Benefit taxes and generality are discussed near the end of this chapter.

3. We do observe this pseudopublicness in many government services areas. Examples include the following: public education, social security, water treatment and sanitation, and many forms of social insurance (which can be general even in cases in which not all within a population receive the service, that is to say that insurance payouts differ, as long as coverage is the same; for example, all would have received the service had the insured contingency arisen, and nearly all would have subscribed to it from behind the Rawlsian veil).

4. The production of many government services with geographical economies of scale in distribution exhibit local diseconomies of geographical scale in production. The servicing and housing of military capital goods are often concentrated on just a few very large bases. Fire trucks and other equipment are based in a few large garages rather than distributed among neighborhoods in small garages. Much of the justice system is housed in a few police departments and court buildings.

Chapter 11: Generality and redistribution

1. The basic analysis presented in this section was originally developed, in somewhat more detail, in James M. Buchanan (1975b).

Chapter 12: Generality without uniformity: Social insurance

1. Not all private lotteries or insurance polices are ex ante general in the sense used here. The likelihood of particular contingencies often varies systematically from person to person. Some individuals are much more likely to be damaged than others because their circumstances differ. Consider the different probabilities of being damaged by a flood or earthquake in Connecticut or California. Lotteries and other games of chance can also be biased toward or away from particular individuals or groups. Such biases are rarely advertised, and are often illegal, but statistical favoritism is clearly possible in both insurance and lotteries.

2. Congleton and Sweetser (1992) provided empirical evidence that uncertainty can facilitate majority decision making concerning the federal budget.

3. It may be argued that a generality constraint for the hypothetical Rawlsian constitutional convention tends to make a social contract more feasible. The more uniformly distributed are the contract benefits, the greater is the expected utility of risk-averse voters. Thus, adherence

to a generality principle might itself be expected to emerge from negotiation behind the veil for a very wide range of public policies.

4. It might be argued that the intuitive appeal of the generality principle is based on cultural norms of fairness.

Chapter 13: Generality without uniformity: Federalism

1. The generality principle effectively rules out differential charges for the same services and different tax rates for those who use more or less of a particular local service. The "benefit" tax result of idealized Tiebout-competition occurs because of fiscal variations among communities rather than fiscal variations within communities.

2. We do observe that local governments nearly always rely upon proportional taxation of a broad tax base (property values) for significant portions of their revenues. Moreover critical services of education, transport, and law enforcement are provided in a more or less uniform manner within most service areas; all this without formal acknowledgment of the merits of generality in most cases.

3. It may be argued that a generality constraint for the hypothetical Rawlsian constitutional convention tends to make a social contract more feasible. The more uniformly distributed are the contract benefits, the greater is the expected utility of risk-averse voters. Thus, adherence to a generality principle might itself be expected to emerge from negotiation behind the veil for a very wide range of public policies.

Chapter 14: The political shape of constitutional order

1. Francis Fukuyama (1992) in *The End of History and the Last Man* made precisely this prediction.

References

Ackerman, Bruce A. 1980. *Social Justice in the Liberal State*. New Haven and London: Yale University Press.

Ames, B., R. Magaw, and L. S. Gold. 1987. Ranking Possible Carcinogenic Hazards. *Science* 236 (No. 4799): 271–280.

Arrow, Kenneth J. 1951. *Social Choice and Individual Values*. New York: Wiley.

Barro, Robert. 1974. Are Government Bonds Net Wealth? *Journal of Political Economy* 82 (November/December): 1095–1118.

Becker, Gary S. 1983. A Theory of Competition among Pressure Groups for Political Influence. *Quarterly Journal of Economics* 98 (No. 3, August): 371–400.

Bhagwati, Jagdish N. 1982. Directly Unproductive Profit-seeking (DUP) Activities. *Journal of Political Economy* 90 (51): 980–1002.

Black, Duncan. 1958. *Theory of Committees and Elections*. Cambridge, England: Cambridge University Press.

Brennan, Geoffrey. 1987. The Case Against Tax Reform. *Critical Issues, No. 7*. Perth, Australia: Australian Institute for Public Policy.

Brennan, Geoffrey, and James Buchanan. 1980. *The Power to Tax*. Cambridge, England: Cambridge University Press.

1981a. The Tax System as Social Overhead Capital: A Constitutional Perspective on Fiscal Norms. In Dieter Biehl, Karl W. Roskamp, and Wolfgang F. Stolper (eds.), *Public Finance and Economic Growth*, 46–56. Detroit, MI: Wayne State University Press.

1981b. The Normative Purpose of Economic "Science": Rediscovery of an Eighteenth Century Method. *International Review of Law and Economics* 1 (December): 15–66.

1983. Predictive Power and Choice Among Regimes. *Economic Journal* 93 (March): 89–105.

Browning, Edgar K. 1975. Why the Social Insurance Budget is Too Large in a Democracy. *Economic Inquiry* 12 (September): 373–388.

Buchanan, James M. 1949. The Pure Theory of Public Finance. *Journal of Political Economy* 57: 496–505.

1954. Social Choice, Democracy, and Free Markets. *Journal of Political Economy* 62 (April): 114–123.

1958. *Public Principles of Public Debt*. Homewood: Irwin.

1964. Fiscal Institutions and Efficiency in Collective Outlay. *American Economic Review* 54 (May): 227–235.

1968. *Demand and Supply of Public Goods*. Chicago: Rand McNally.

1975a. *The Limits of Liberty: Between Anarchy and Leviathan*. Chicago: University of Chicago Press.

1975b. The Political Economy of Franchise in the Welfare State. In R. T. Selden (ed.), *Capitalism and Freedom: Problems and Prospects*, 52–77. Charlottesville: University Press of Virginia.

1976. Taxation in Fiscal Exchange. *Journal of Public Economics* 6: 17–29.

1989. The Relatively Absolute Absolutes. In *Essays on the Political Economy*, 32–46. Honolulu: University of Hawaii Press.

1993a. How Can Constitutions Be Designed So That Politicians Who Seek to Serve Public Interest Can Survive? *Constitutional Political Economy* 4 (No. 1, Winter): 1–6.

1993b. The Political Efficiency of General Taxation. *National Tax Journal* 46 (No. 4): 401–410.

1995a. Foundational Concerns: A Criticism of Public Choice Theory. In José Casas Pardo and Friedrich Schneider (eds.), *Current Issues in Public Choice*, 3–20. Cheltenham, England: Edward Elgar.

1995b. *Majoritarian Rent Seeking*. Center for Study of Public Choice, George Mason University, Fairfax, Virginia, working paper.

1996. *Rule Feasibility and Rule Dominance*. Center for Study of Public Choice, George Mason University, Fairfax, Virginia, working paper.

1997. Majoritarian Logic. *Public Choice*.

Buchanan, James M., and Dwight R. Lee. 1982. Tax Rates and Tax Revenues in Political Equilibrium: Some Simple Analytics. *Economic Inquiry* 20 (July): 344–354.

1991. Cartels, Coalitions, and Constitutional Politics. *Constitutional Political Economy* 2 (No. 2, Spring/Summer): 139–161. Originally published in *Public Choice Studies* 13 (1989): 5–20. [Japanese translation]

Buchanan, James M., Charles K. Rowley, and Robert D. Tollison (eds.). 1987. *Deficits*. New York: Blackwell.

Buchanan, James M., Robert D. Tollison, and Gordon Tullock (eds.). 1980. *Towards a Theory of the Rent-Seeking Society*. College Station: Texas A&M University Press.

Buchanan, James M., and Gordon Tullock. 1962. *The Calculus of Consent: Logical Foundations of Constitutional Democracy*. Ann Arbor: University of Michigan Press.

Buchanan, James M., and Yong J. Yoon. 1995. Rational Majoritarian Taxation of the Rich: With Increasing Returns and Capital Accumulation. *Southern Economic Journal* 61 (No. 4, April): 923–935.

Coleman, Jules. 1985. Market Contractarianism and the Unanimity Rule. *Social Philosophy and Policy* 2: 69–114.

Congleton, Roger D. 1994. Constitutional Federalism and Decentralization. *Economia Delle Scelte Pubbliche* (No. 1): 15–30.

Congleton, Roger D. (ed.). 1996. *The Political Economy of Environmental Protection*. Ann Arbor: University of Michigan Press.

Congleton, Roger D., and William Shughart. 1990. The Growth of Social Security Expenditures, Electoral Push or Political Pull? *Economic Inquiry* 28 (No. 1, January): 109–132.

Congleton, Roger D., and W. Sweetser. 1992. The Value of the Veil: How Much Distributional Information Is Enough? *Public Choice* 73: 1–19.

Congleton, Roger D., and Robert D. Tollison. 1996. *The Stable Individual Properties of Instability*. Center for Study of Public Choice, George Mason University, working paper.

Cornes, R., and T. Sandler. 1996. *The Theory of Externalities, Public Goods, and Club Goods*, 2nd ed. New York: Cambridge University Press.

Cropper, M., W. N. Evans, S. J. Berardi, M. M. Duela Soares, and P. Portney. 1992. The Determinants of Pesticide Regulation: A Statistical Analysis of EPA Decision Making. *Journal of Political Economy* 100 (No. 1): 175–197.

de Jasay, Anthony. 1985. *The State*. Oxford: Basil Blackwell.

Demsetz, Harold. 1967. Toward a Theory of Property Rights. *American Economic Review, Papers and Proceedings* 57 (No. 2): 347–359.

Elster, Jon. 1979. *Ulysses and the Sirens: Studies in Rationality and Irrationality*. New York: Cambridge University Press.

Flowers, Marilyn R., and Patricia M. Danzon. 1984. Separation of the Redistributive and Allocative Functions of Government: A Public Choice Perspective. *Journal of Public Economics* 24 (No. 3): 373–380.

Fukuyama, Francis. 1992. *The End of History and the Last Man*. New York: Free Press.

Habermas, Jürgen. 1983. *Moralbewusstsein und kommunikatives Handeln*. Frankfurt, Germany: Suhrkamp. [Awareness of Morality and Interactive Communication]

Hall, Robert E., and Alvin Rabushka. 1983. *Low Tax, Simple Tax, Flat Tax*. New York: McGraw-Hill.

Harsanyi, John. 1955. Cardinal Welfare, Individualistic Ethics, and Interpersonal Comparisons of Utility. *Journal of Political Economy* 63 (August): 309–321.

Hayek, F. A. 1960. *The Constitution of Liberty*. Chicago: University of Chicago Press.

Hobbes, Thomas. 1943. *Leviathan*. London: Everymans Library. Originally published in 1651.

Hochman, Harold M., and James D. Rodgers. 1969. Pareto Optimal Redistribution. *American Economic Review* Part 1, 59 (No. 4, September): 542–557.

Hoyt, William H., and Eugenia F. Toma. 1989. State Mandates and Interest Group Lobbying. *Journal of Public Economics* 38 (No. 2, March): 199–213.

Kliemt, Hartmut. 1995. Rule of Law and the Welfare State. *Philosophica* 56: 121–132.

Krueger, Anne O. 1974. The Political Economy of the Rent-Seeking Society. *American Economic Review* 64 (June): 291–303.

Lee, Dwight R., and Arthur Snow. 1993. *Political Incentives and Optimal Excess Burden*. University of Georgia, working paper.

Leoni, Bruno. 1961. *Freedom and the Law*. Princeton: Van Nostrand.

Levy, David. 1995. *Stigler's Revival of Mandeville*. Center for Study of Public Choice, George Mason University, working paper.

Lindahl, Erik. 1919. *Die Gerechtigkeit der Besteuerung*. Lund, Sweden: Gleerupska Universitets–Bokhandeln. [Justice of Taxation]

  1967. Just Taxation – A Positive Solution. In Richard A. Musgrave and Alan T. Peacock (eds.), *Classics in the Theory of Public Finance*, 168–176. New York: St. Martin's Press. Chapter originally published in 1919.

Locke, John. 1955. *Second Treatise of Civil Government*. Chicago: Gateway. Originally published in 1689.

Magee, Stephen P., William A. Brock, and Leslie Young.1989. *Black Hole Tariffs and Endogenous Policy Theory*. Cambridge, England: Cambridge University Press.

Meyer, Arthur B. 1966. Forests and Forestry. In Henry Clepper (ed.), *Origins of American Conservation*, 38–56. New York: Ronald Press.

Musgrave, Richard A. 1959. *The Theory of Public Finance*. New York: McGraw-Hill.

Musgrave, Richard A., and Alan T. Peacock (eds.). 1967. *Classics in the Theory of Public Finance*. New York: St. Martin's Press.

Oates, W. 1972. *Fiscal Federalism*. New York: Harcourt Brace Jovanovich.

Ostrom, E. 1990. *Governing the Commons: The Evolution of Institutions for Collective Action*. New York: Cambridge University Press.

Posner, Richard. 1972. *Economic Analysis of Law*. Boston: Little, Brown.

Rawls, John. 1971. *A Theory of Justice*. Cambridge, MA: Harvard University Press.

Ricardo, David. 1933. *On Principles of Political Economy and Taxation*. New York: E. P. Dutton. Originally published in 1817.

Samuelson, Paul A. 1954. The Pure Theory of Public Expenditure. *Review of Economics and Statistics* 36 (November): 387–389.

Sen, Amartya K. 1970. The Impossibility of a Paretian Liberal. *Journal of Political Economy* 78 (January–February): 152–157.

Shepsle, Kenneth A., and Barry R. Weingast. 1981. Structure Induced Equilibrium and Legislative Choice. *Public Choice* 37 (No. 3): 503–519.

Smith, Adam. 1937. *The Wealth of Nations*. New York: Modern Library Edition. Originally published in 1776.

Sopper, William E. 1966. Watershed Management. In Henry Clepper (ed.), *Origins of American Conservation*, 101–118. New York: Ronald Press.

Sraffa, Piero (ed.). 1951. *Works and Correspondence of David Ricardo* (Vol. 1, 244–249; Vol. 4, 149–200). Cambridge, England: Cambridge University Press.

Tiebout, Charles M. 1956. A Pure Theory of Local Expenditure. *Journal of Political Economy* 64 (No. 5, October): 416–424.

Tollison, Robert D. 1997. Rent Seeking. In Dennis C. Mueller (ed.), *Perspectives in Public Choice: A Handbook*, 506–525. Cambridge, England: Cambridge University Press.

Tollison, Robert D., and Roger D. Congleton (eds.). 1995. *The Economic Analysis of Rent Seeking*. London: Edward Elgar.

Tuerck, David A. 1967. Constitutional Asymmetry. *Papers in Non-Market Decision Making* 2: 27–44.

Tullock, Gordon. 1967. The Welfare Costs of Tariffs, Monopolies, and Theft. *Western Economic Journal* 5 (June): 224–232.

1981. Why So Much Stability? *Public Choice* 37 (2): 189–202.

Vanberg, Viktor, and James M. Buchanan. 1989. Interests and Theories in Constitutional Choice. *Journal of Theoretical Politics* 1 (No. 1, January): 49–62.

von Neumann, John, and Oskar Morgenstern. 1944. *Theory of Games and Economic Behavior*. Princeton: Princeton University Press.

Wicksell, Knut. 1896. *Finanztheoretische Untersuchungen*. Jena, Germany: Fischer. Theoretical Analyses in Public Finance.

1967. A New Principle of Just Taxation. In R. A. Musgrave and A. T. Peacock (eds.), *Classics in the Theory of Public Finance*, 72–118. New York: St. Martin's Press. Chapter originally published in 1896.

Index

165